H. Page Williams

DOING MYSELF A FAVOR:

LOVING MY WIFE

BRIDGE PUBLISHING
South Plainfield, NJ

Doing Myself a Favor: Loving My Wife
    by H. Page Williams
ISBN 0-88270-664-0
Library of Congress Catalog Card #94-070703
Copyright © 1994 by Patti Williams

Published by:
Bridge Publishing Inc.
2500 Hamilton Blvd.
South Plainfield, NJ 07080

Printed in the United States of America.
All rights reserved under International Copyright
Law. Contents and/or cover may not be repro-
duced in whole or in part in any form without the
express written consent of the Publisher.

Contents

Preface

In writing *Doing Myself a Favor: Loving My Wife*, I wanted to say something to and for "ordinary" people. I have received hundreds of letters and phone calls from ordinary people who have read the book I wrote in 1973, *Do Yourself a Favor: Love Your Wife*, a book that has sold approximately 500,000 copies. Men let me know about the positive impact the book made on their lives, their marriages and their families.

My main concern in writing this sequel is that the thoughts and words I use in this book will be enabled by the power of God's Spirit to touch your life and inspire you to a nobler life in Christ and a happier home life.

Most books, both sacred and secular, tend to concentrate on the sensational aspects of life. Most of us are not criminals, members of some remote tribe of cannibals, or terminal cancer patients. Likewise, most of us are not celebrities. Many of today's popular Christian books, however, tell stories about these sorts of people. But what about the men and women who live under much more ordinary circumstances? One would almost think that in order to be a successful disciple of Christ, you first have to be an alcoholic, drug addict, Satan worshiper or at least have a brush with the law.

If that is true, then most of us are "sunk." Or are we? We may not participate in gang wars, but some of our family feuds arouse emotions that are no less intense. We may not rob banks, but our secret motives and desires—if they ever came to the surface—might embarrass us more deeply than being arrested for holding up the local savings and loan. We are not cannibals, except in the sense that we bite and devour one another with our gossip, sarcasm and criticism.

In fact, every one of us desperately needs Jesus Christ because each one of us is a sinner. Fortunately for us, the Kingdom of God is open to sinners only. And we ordinary people are likely to fool ourselves into believing that we're not sinners—that we don't really need the grace and mercy of God in Christ Jesus.

Christianity is much more than just Bible reading, prayer and church attendance. It permeates into the concrete business and details of daily living. The question does not concern how I behave in public. Most of us are trained in social graces and act decently enough in a restaurant or church. The real issue of Christian life regards, for example, how I act and feel in the morning when my spouse or child ties up the bathroom and I'm compelled to wait!

We've known for a long time that man looks on our outward appearance, while God looks on our hearts. (See 1 Sam. 16:7.) Helpless to change our hearts, we've had to become "practical atheists" and concentrate on modifying our behavior. It's a pity that some of us try so hard, instead of trusting in the power of God's Spirit to engage us in supernatural living. Our Herculean efforts to control our personal lives and the lives of our family count for nothing. The realization of this angers us because we have been in denial too long.

To God alone be the glory as your awareness of these truths heightens to the point where you will desire to hear the best *news* any person will ever hear—Jesus can and does change our hearts and lives. The following chapters are formed from incidents out of my own story which indicates that *Doing Myself a Favor: Loving My Wife* is a continuing process.

It is not my purpose in the first three chapters of this book to duplicate *The Confessions of St. Augustine*. Rather, I want to let you see some of my own misguided behavior patterns and attitudes. Hopefully, you will identify with some of them, and in so doing, the Holy Spirit can convict your heart and create in you a desire to change and grow in your relationship with God, your wife and your family.

1

Collision Course

The blue-and-white Cessna 150 taxied to the end of the runway. It was a cloudless day over Cairo, Georgia, and Patti and I basked in the sunshine as we stood, arm in arm, waving good-bye. Soon the little plane was airborne. The pilot circled to fly back over the field. He tipped his wing in a last good-bye as he passed over us and then soared into the deep blue sky. Our prayers went with the couple in the plane as they headed into a new and exciting phase of marriage, after twenty-five years of traveling along a bumpy path together.

Steve and Carol had been our overnight guests. We had spent sixteen hours in intensive counseling with them. Their marriage was falling apart at the seams when they arrived, and they were both desperate—truly desperate. This is probably why it only took sixteen hours! But the night before, as we sat down together and began to talk, Steve was still ready to "bail out" of his marriage. He complained, "Page, it's easy for you and Patti to have a good marriage

1

because you've never had any problems!"

I smiled and replied, "Steve, what Patti and I have today is a miracle. We tend to forget what it takes in terms of pressure, cutting and polishing to produce a fine diamond. And like diamonds, fine marriages don't just sprout up naturally. If our marriage had been left alone to grow up by itself, my hypocrisy, rebellion, pride and self-righteousness would have destroyed it long ago."

Steve looked skeptical. He couldn't believe that I possessed such traits. We had met before casually and he had seen only the mask I usually wear in public, the mask of the warm and friendly pastor, the humble servant of Jesus. I knew I'd have to be more honest with him, so I gave him an accurate thumbnail sketch of what I had really amounted to as a husband and father—until I got into such deep trouble that I cried out to Jesus for help. As Steve listened to the story of my failure and God's faithfulness, relief, followed by hope, began to show in his eyes. The way was opening up for us to get down to the business of helping these two frightened people find God's help for their own marriage.

Patti and I have seen it happen countless times. We have met people from every walk of life whose marriages have been on the rocks because they weren't on the Rock. When we've had the opportunity to share our story, they've frequently been helped because they've seen that God blessed us—not for being good, but for being willing to change. Let me clarify that right at the outset. I use the term "us" loosely, but the critical matter for the success of our marriage was that "I" would be willing to change. To find out

2

why that was and is true, you'll have to read the rest of this book.

"I'll Bet Your Husband Sure Does Enjoy You!"

Some years ago, an elderly gentleman rang the doorbell of our new home in Columbus, Georgia. We were just settling in after moving from our previous church in Florida. The gentleman's name was Mr. Poor. He was the local printer who came by to pick up the material for the Sunday bulletin. He hadn't met my wife, Patti, and when she came to the door, his eyes widened at the petite and attractive blond who stood before him. Speechless for a moment, he finally quipped, "I'll bet your husband sure does enjoy you!"

He was right! It had not always been so, however. Some years before that, Patti and I had been in the midst of a heated argument. Neither of us was pulling any punches. At one point, she accused me of something very bad. I hated to hear Patti make such an accusation; at the same moment, I intensely hated her for saying it. I was caught. Never before had I been willing to admit how much anger I felt toward her, but now I blurted it out. I was startled at my own honesty, but Patti, as much as it hurt her to hear it, was not startled at all. She had known it for a long time. I was the one who was not willing to face it. I had refused to see myself as anything but a congenial and loving person.

But now it was out. I *loathed* my wife, the one person I had vowed before God and man to love, honor and cherish. What would happen now? Would I be struck dead? Would Patti leave me? Would I be disqualified as a pastor? The idol I had created of myself had been broken into pieces. My world—a little kingdom of self—was in ruins.

Thankfully, this was not the end but only the beginning. The tension of the fight left us, and soon we were talking—really sharing—for one of the first times in our marriage. Patti set her pain aside and began to help me go back into my childhood to discover the root of my anger. I began to express feelings—hurt, bitterness, vindictiveness, lust—that I had long repressed and denied. At least, I liked to think I had repressed them. Actually, they had a way of coming up pretty persistently whenever my guard was down. Subconsciously, I was always looking for an excuse to vent my spleen on somebody; most often, it was my children or my wife. After all, the kids weren't big enough to strike back, and Patti, I reasoned, wouldn't turn me in because she loved me (which, in my thinking, meant that she adored and worshiped me and would never cross me in word or deed).

A "Very Good" Little Boy

As we looked at my past, I began to see the present more clearly. My mother had married my father when she was only fifteen, and he was nearly twice her age. After three children and several unhappy years together, they divorced, and my mother married my father's brother, my uncle. I was three at the time. After four more children, my stepfather died of cancer of the esophagus, which I'm convinced had something to do with his outlook on life and consequent heavy drinking and smoking.

I enjoyed being the "baby," and it seems I've spent most of my life trying to stay in that category. As I

4

look back on my earlier years, I must have subconsciously seen them as a place of warmth, love and security, with no attendant responsibilities. Pure bliss!

Of course, fighting to stay in babyhood was a losing battle. But I was tenacious about it. Even after I turned in my bottle and diapers, I kept doing things to keep the adoring affection of my parents. To me that meant being "very good." But it didn't work. Even if my parents had been perfect, they could not have given me what I was wanting. Those were the days following the Depression, and my parents had too many other problems to give me much extra attention, let alone the uninterrupted adulation I was looking for.

Needless to say, I went off to public school pretty much in a huff. But hope springs eternal, and I was optimistic that just around the corner was the girl who would take the place of my "mother." Although these were not conscious thoughts, looking back on my life and the lack of love I felt from my parents, I recognized that these factors had a lot to do with my selfish and unhealthy outlook of life.

As Patti and I talked on, I began to pour out more and more things that I had bottled up for many years. A repressed memory of an incident that occurred when I was about nine years old came back to me. I had been deeply jealous and resentful when my grandmother wrapped up an erector set to send off to an orphanage right before my very eyes. I thought she had bought the erector set, something I had desired for some time, just for *me*. I actually wept then, although I didn't understand why, until Patti and I talked about it. I was nine years old at the time of the incident, and I quickly wiped those tears away. Then

5

I told my grandmother how happy I was for the little orphan who would soon be playing with that erector set. That's what I figured she wanted me to say. After all, she and grandad were solid members of the First Baptist Church. The gift was for the church project, and I would win their approval if I displayed a proper, generous attitude. Hypocrisy had already become a way of life for me. I knew how to put on an act in order to perform as others wanted me to.

As Patti helped me to see the truth about my relationship with my grandparents, something even more disturbing came to light. My parents never went to church. My brothers and sisters went sometimes, but I was there every Sunday with my grandparents. It began to make sense. Grandparents are always more willing to dote on a youngster than his parents are. I must have figured that I had better prospects of getting what I was looking for from them than I ever would from mom and dad.

The First Baptist Church of Ft. Pierce, Florida, my grandparents' church, was then the largest and most prestigious church in town. I usually sat in the third pew from the front on the preacher's right, and since my grandparents weren't too strict about it, I usually managed a little nap there in the third pew each Sunday morning. After his sermon, the minister would come down in front of the pulpit to invite people to come forward to receive Christ. As he did so, the congregation would sing a suitable hymn. One morning, as we were singing the invitational hymn, I left the pew and arrived in front of the minister, barefooted and with tears streaming down my cheeks. The preacher shook my little hand—he seemed like a giant to me—and I was converted as I "professed" my faith in Christ.

6

Looking back on that day, Patti and I began to put some ideas together. The Sunday of my conversion came not long after that incident with the erector set. I was hurt and no doubt realized that my grandparents weren't going to fulfill my fantasies any more than my parents had. But, still trying to get their "approval," I went forward to give my heart to Jesus, hoping this would please my grandparents. Like I said, hope springs eternal.

Anyway, I was baptized that evening. The baptism symbolized my problem since my grandparents were in charge of the baptismal candidates. I emerged from those waters of death and new life with Christ, and ran straight into their arms as they helped me out of my wet clothes and into dry ones so that I could rejoin the congregation for the rest of the service. Today I can only shudder to think of my effrontery. I was in a sense asking God to take me on my terms which meant, first, that I wanted Him to serve me, and second, that I wanted my grandparents to be "co-saviors" with Him. It was merciful of the Lord to take me that day just as I was—not on my terms, but on the tiny toehold I had actually given to Him. Then He patiently set to work to save me from my self-pity and idolatry—two killers of true spirituality.

Building My Image

However, it was a long time before I ever gave Him much more than that little toehold to work on. As much as anything, I began to look back on my conversion with a feeling that was smug and self-righteous. I spent most of my time in succeeding years building my image. I did everything I could to convince my relatives and friends of how wonderful I was. Some people—the ones who did not know me too well—actually believed me. In high school, for example, I was elected the "most intellectual" member of my class. Actually, my grades weren't anything spectacular (I had even failed fifth grade), but I made a practice of walking around the campus with a pile of books under each arm. After all, if you can't *be* good, you must at least try to *look* good!

Maintaining my act was an enormous strain. Always lurking just beneath the surface was that angry little baby. Talk about touchy! Before Patti and I were married, we were dating regularly by the time I was a senior and she was a junior at Fort Pierce High. I hung around her house a lot. She was so good-looking and sweet. Maybe this time I had at last succeeded in my great quest for a "savior-mother." But, after my two big letdowns with mom and grandma, I was wary.

One Sunday I invited myself over to her house for dinner. After the meal, we were alone in the kitchen together, washing and drying the dinner dishes. In a moment of amorous presumption, I reached over to kiss Patti on the cheek, but she moved away. Ouch! It was just as I feared. I was rejected—spurned by my true love.

Actually, Patti had only stepped aside to put some dishes in the cabinet. She had been totally unaware of my romantic progress behind her back. But I couldn't pay any attention to that. This was too good an opportunity to give vent to my self-pity. In fact, I spent a lot of my time looking for excuses to pout. It felt so good. It's a wonder that my lower lip didn't begin to resemble Pinocchio's nose!

One day, after Patti graduated from high school, she and her mother and I were having lunch at a local restaurant. As usual, I was feeling hurt about something and I was casting a gloomy shadow over the otherwise pleasant meal. Patti had long since given up trying to coax me out of my little moods. But on this day, she took a positive step in the other direction. She purposefully removed the engagement ring I had given her from her third finger, tossed it on the table, and stared straight into my eyes, "Page, I won't marry a man who acts the way you do!" Her voice wasn't angry, but it was firm. And, in a small measure, it brought me to my senses.

I straightened up, apologized and promised to reform. It was a sobering slap in my face in the best sense of the word. "Thanks, I needed that." But, like an alcoholic, I didn't stay sober long. That one little threat only made me modify my behavior slightly, but it didn't change my heart. I went into marriage still hoping to get the idolatrous adoration I wanted from Patti. In my fantasy, I saw her orbiting dutifully around me in the dual roles of doting mother and purring sex kitten. The role she played would depend upon my mood and expectations at any given moment.

Enfant Terrible

Of course, I didn't see myself in this light then. Instead of His Majesty, H. Page Williams, *enfant terrible,* I presented myself as warm and lovable Page, a slightly mistreated fellow for whom you ought to feel a bit sorry. I had studied this role from early childhood. By the time I was in grammar school, I had it down pat so that in my school picture I looked exactly like an escapee from Boy's Town.

My act even helped me once in a commercial venture. I sold parched peanuts one summer to the train passengers at the Fort Pierce train station. Whenever a train rolled in, I would dash along the tracks shouting, "Peanuts! Peanuts! Get your peanuts. Grown in the shade, parched in the sun, get yours now or you won't get none!" I did a land-office business and, at the time, I attributed it to my Madison Avenue jingle. But now that I think about it, those train passengers probably felt sorry for me. It may even have given them a good feeling—as if they had contributed to a charity—to buy parched peanuts from the little uncombed, barefoot urchin with his dirty face and skinned knees. (I fell down a lot on that train platform running after customers.) I guess my real sales approach was more sophisticated and powerful than I realized.

I began to feel like an orphan very early in life. I was born in 1934, but my birth was not a welcomed event. My parents were not looking for another mouth to feed when it was almost impossible to feed the other two kids they already had—my five-year-old brother and three-year-old sister. Dad was so shaken by my arrival that he went out and got drunk. Of course I didn't know this at the time, but babies feel things like rejection. And, as the years passed, that feeling was reinforced. It made me mad, but I was too little to punish my parents for not wanting me, so I turned my anger inward and just felt sorry for myself.

This set my course for life. Even before I entered school, I had developed a pattern of getting hurt in a vain effort to get my parents' attention and maybe even get them to feel sorry for the way they treated me. I almost drowned. I set the woods on fire. I frequently fell out of trees and other high places. Once I was nearly killed when I landed on concrete, head-first.

In 1943, I was nine years old and making good money as a shoeshine boy for the sailors at the Fort Pierce Naval Base. I could really pop that polishing rag, and when I put on a little extra show with the job, I usually got a tip in addition to the regular ten-cent fee. I was pretty pleased with myself until one day my balloon was burst again. I was busy polishing a sailor's shoes, and I happened to look up at the sailor. He grinned and said, "Son, you'd better pin your ears back before you fly away!" I repressed the feeling of hurt, and it was years before I was able to deal with it.

Another thing that made me mad was the way my parents would applaud my older brother's efforts, but not mine. I did everything he did. He delivered papers, so did I. He played in the high school band, so I joined too. He made good grades, which I tried to do as well, although that was tougher. He was going to go to college, so I decided that's what I'd do. But none of this ever impressed my folks.

Actually, my life was not nearly as gloomy as I liked to think. I made enough money shining shoes to buy war bonds, which I used to help my parents buy some property. That made me feel pretty good. On Saturdays I would rake the back yard, for which I was paid a dime. In the afternoon, I'd spend my dime to see the latest western at the movie theater and get a penny's worth of candy. I especially liked Johnny Mack Brown because he didn't sing or kiss the girls.

When I was thirteen, I got to help my stepfather and his brother (who was the carpenter) build our house from scratch. It was a five-man crew: my stepfather, his brother (my uncle), his son (my cousin), my older brother and me. There were plenty of pine trees on some other property my stepfather owned, and we used them to build the house. Although I helped with many aspects of building our house, my biggest job was to clear the property. Using only a hoe, I grubbed four lots filled with palmetto bushes that had huge, tough root systems. Even now as I remember it, I can smell the strong odor of the broken earth and feel the pain of my aching arms and back. I can see the blisters on my hands and hear the sound of the sharp grubbing hoe as it cut through the roots and earth. It would have been hard labor for a grown man. I can remember the satisfaction I felt at the end of each day, looking at the cleared ground and pile of palmettos ready to be burned or hauled off to the dump. I really felt proud to be a part of the team, and I was proud of the house we built.

Another thing that made me feel grown-up was hunting for quail and doves. My stepfather was an expert marksman, and he always had two or three bird-dogs known as pointers. The quail were plentiful and they made a delicious meal, especially the way my mother cooked them. It really made me feel like a "big shot" when I could fire off our big, double-barreled, ten-gauge shotgun without getting knocked down by the recoil. But even before that day came, I was a determined hunter and bagged myself many doves with that cannon. The trouble was that I never knew for sure if I had hit my game until I picked myself up off the ground and hunted around the foot of the tree where the dove had innocently perched before I shot at it.

My stepfather—though he was frighteningly violent when he was intoxicated, as he often was—was kind to me and frequently took me hunting and fishing. He was quite an outdoorsman and, even when money was scarce, we usually had fresh fish, game or fowl on the table. So my life was not the unmitigated disaster I portrayed to others.

Probably my most real deprivation was in my relationship with my father and stepfather. I never really knew them. They were both cold and distant—they probably didn't have any better idea of what it meant to be a whole person, a husband or a father than I did when I got married.

2

A Darn Good Husband

The Best Little Christian You Ever Saw

Actually, I changed dramatically after I joined my grandparents' church. Now, instead of being alternately well-behaved and insanely accident-prone, I concentrated all my efforts on being—make that "looking"—very, very good. I honestly felt like "little Jack Horner." I was the best little Christian you ever saw; at least that's what I thought.

In high school I was elected to various class and student body offices. I was elected band captain. I taught a Sunday school class and led the singing at church. At school I got a whole pocketful of awards and honors. I must have had the most swollen ego in my little hometown of Ft. Pierce. I had convinced myself what a good boy I was. I failed, however, to convince anyone at home. They knew me too well.

In addition to all my school and church activities, I worked almost incessantly. My first job was gutting fish in one of the canneries down near the Indian River. That was short-lived. My next job was with the

15

local newspaper. I was a delivery boy. Then I worked in a locksmith's shop and, in turn, a lawn-mower repair shop and then with an air-conditioner firm, installing air-conditioners. I worked with my uncle Ernest at a nearby packing house (fruit business) for several years making orange crates. During one long summer, I helped my stepfather drive his eighteen-wheeler rig all over the eastern United States.

One person who had a strong, positive influence on me during those days was a school teacher named Dwight West. Mr. West had been handicapped as a child by polio. I often chauffeured him around in his Chevy. We had lots of good talks during our rides together. He, in many ways, pointed me toward the ministry.

But none of these things, not even all of them put together, outweighed my intense interest in a pretty band majorette named Patti McGauran. She played clarinet in the high school band, and I played the French horn. We sat at just the right angle for me to do a little winking and flirting during band practice. I felt that she was the cutest, smartest and most talented girl in Ft. Pierce High School. I put all of my energies to work to impress her with the idea that I would make a wonderful husband. It wasn't that I succeeded, but rather that God knew just the person I needed for a life partner to accomplish His purposes later.

"They Tried to Tell Us We're Too Young"

In 1953, Patti and my folks tearfully waved good-bye as I left Ft. Pierce on a Greyhound bus headed for Deland, Florida, where Stetson University was located. I was entering as a ministerial student, for I had recently felt called to prepare for the gospel ministry. I was not a very likely candidate, but nonetheless, "God moves in mysterious ways, His wonders to perform," as Cowper so beautifully stated. In 1955, less than a year after Patti finished high school, we got married. Both of us were too young. In fact, that was the year Nat King Cole made famous his ballad, "They Tried To Tell Us We're Too Young," which we adopted as our theme song.

I was sure that marriage would bring me all I had been looking for—all I had felt deprived of since early childhood, especially the feeling of physical closeness. I was not prepared to take a wife. I didn't have a clue as to what being a husband entailed. Instead, I was a child who at last had found an opportunity to be coddled. In addition, Patti would bring in money and be able to help keep me in college. Admittedly, these were not very high-minded motives for marriage or anything else, for that matter.

But I wasn't looking at such things then. I saw myself as a "darn good husband." To start with, I read Geisseman's *Make Yours a Happy Marriage* the night before our wedding. That, I was sure, would make me a pro, ready for anything. Our pastor tried to warn me that marriage was not a bowl of cherries, but nobody could tell me anything. My ego was too big for that.

The Bible says pride goes before destruction. Probably the first time I clearly experienced the destructive capacity of my egotism was in our little apartment near Stetson University. Patti and I were both students, and we both worked. One evening I came home and, as usual, the table was set and dinner was ready to be served. Patti set out the succotash, salad, warm rolls and iced tea. I thought to myself, "Where are the potatoes?" After all, *my mother always served potatoes with succotash.*

Patti must have realized something was bothering me. I was looking around the kitchen. "Is anything wrong, Page?" Patti inquired.

Without thinking about the consequences, I demanded, "Where are the potatoes? My mom always has potatoes." I continued with my harangue, adding more fuel to the fire. I exposed my real feelings (which I usually hid) and without realizing it, the feelings peeped out over the edge of my "good boy" battlements and I think Patti got a fair first look at the real Page. I have to tell you, she was not a happy camper. In fact, she was justifiably indignant and told me so in no uncertain words. In fact, she "pitched a fit!" Her eyes got as big as saucers and her voice as high as G-sharp, and after telling me a few things, she dashed out of the kitchen into the big over-stuffed chair in the living room and sobbed.

What had I done? All I said was, "Where's the potatoes?" Although this was only our first spat, divorce was conceivable to me because I felt our marriage was falling apart. Patti was beginning to see, however dimly, that I had conned her. Years later, when her vision had sharpened considerably, she told me that she had married an "optical illusion."

If you have an ego as big as mine was, even slightly harsh words are unbearable. I felt that Patti had exploded unreasonably, covering me with undeserved abuse. So, of course I was furious that she would have the gall to attack "wonderful me." But when you're as wonderful as I was, you don't bring your anger out on the line. Instead I acted very politely, while inside

I branded Patti as a monster and promised myself never to bother her with things like expressing my thoughts like that again. No use telling her her faults, I reasoned, she couldn't handle it! I would only get her all worked up.

I reasoned to myself that "what she didn't know wouldn't hurt her." But I didn't see how vindictive I was being. Already I was beginning to express hatred toward Patti. I ignored that, however, and still thought myself to be a "darn good husband." After all, I had very nicely been willing to drop the whole matter of the "potato caper" for the sake of peace and quiet in our home (which "the roaring monster" might disturb at any moment if I didn't treat her *just* right).

This whole routine served my purposes very well, but it had devastating effects on our marriage. I was not honest with Patti, especially when it came to her faults (or what I perceived to be her faults). I acted as if she had none (though, of course, I regarded her secretly in the most terrible light). That's the way we "self-righteous men" are. In time, this duplicity put unimaginable strains on the foundations of our relationship. Only the grace of God kept that meager foundation from shattering into a thousand fragments.

Mr. Wonderful

Another way I managed to make myself look better than Patti was by letting her speak her mind on something. I, in turn, would act as if I were perfectly aloof from such worldly strife. This often happened when we would return home from a trying social occasion. Both of us usually felt about the same. For example, our host and hostess might have been offensive in some matter, leaving us feeling irritated. I'd let Patti express the irritation while I gave the impression that I was too good to get irritated or critical. In this way I could coach Patti into accepting her role as monster and I could maintain my role as "Mr. Wonderful." She felt awful, and I felt superior.

Because I was creating this fantasy on such a large scale, much of my thought life became absorbed in fantasy about my greatness and sexual prowess. It would ruin my act to share it with Patti, so I kept my mouth shut. In fact, I became a lousy conversationalist, but I told myself I was the quiet and thoughtful type.

By keeping it all in my head, I could also "compare" myself to other less-hidden husbands and thereby cast more favorable light on myself. Those husbands mistreated their wives, but not precious Page. They squandered their money on camping equipment or the paraphernalia of their favorite sports. Not Page. They spent their evenings with the boys, playing cards and drinking. Not Page. Some of them were adulterers. Not ol' Page (except in his fantasy world). I regularly congratulated myself that I was not like other men. It made me feel good and it soothed a lot of the misgivings I had about my "thought life."

Patti was really lucky to have such a fine husband. This was often reinforced by the ladies of the church when Patti would say something which might suggest that I was not the world's best husband. They would point out to her all the wonderful ways in which I was better than most men. This did not set well with Patti because she knew a lot more about me than they would ever know. You know, the "optical illusion."

All of my perverted thinking continued to feed my fantasy. Since I was so nice—as proved by my comparison of myself to other men's actions—and Patti was so lucky, I could reasonably *blame* her whenever I felt she didn't seem to adequately appreciate me. By my standards (I was looking for total, abject adoration in a perpetual vigil before my shrine), it had become clear that Patti failed to do this with outrageous frequency. Thus I found more fuel for my burning resentment against her. You probably know me well enough by now to know that I didn't directly express this resentment. I was a "darn good husband," so I just stuck my hands deep into my pockets and felt very sorry for myself.

It's Not My Fault!

That wasn't the only thing I blamed Patti for. Whenever anything went wrong, it was not my fault. I always found someone or something else to blame. The most likely candidate for this unenviable post was—you guessed it—Patti. For example, in those early years we usually bought whatever Patti said she wanted. This worked very well because it made me look like a "darn good husband," while I could secretly blame our money troubles on my extravagant wife. I did not mention this to her, however. It helped my case a lot when I remembered my wife's mother saying about Patti—"she is never without want!" I latched on to that concept like a bulldog and would not let it go.

It was on this point of money that my fantasy began to be invaded by a spearhead of reality. After a while, my game backfired and I was deeply in debt! I had to do something, but what? I couldn't be honest. I couldn't afford not to look like a nice guy. I couldn't be wrong. It was rough, but I figured out a way. I turned over the financial management of our household to Patti. She would soon see that we were buying things we didn't need, like frilly curtains, throw rugs, knick-knacks, picture frames, studio portraits of the children and so on. You can be certain that those things were always her idea, not mine.

I thought it was a foolproof plan and that Patti would soon be on both knees before me, begging my forgiveness for her extravagant ways. I dreamt of that moment for some time, but it never occurred. Instead, Patti took over unhesitatingly, and her air of confidence over her new assignment greatly annoyed me. Under her supervision, our financial condition gradually improved, and I was stuck with my self-pity again.

Sex was another source of self-pity. I had gone into marriage thinking that it would give me an immediate and unlimited sexual outlet. You know, "anytime, anyplace!" But I soon discovered that Patti was a person, not a thing or a machine to be used. That made me mad. Then I began to use my anger for my own devices. Whenever Patti failed to respond to me sexually—for whatever reason—I would pout. In that pouting I could conjure up many excuses for my own adulterous fantasy life. After all, if Patti didn't satisfy me, I'd have to go elsewhere!

I also worked hard trying to brainwash Patti on this account. I wanted her to feel guilty because her libido was no match for mine (the truth was that there was nothing wrong with her libido; it's just not always fun to make love with an egomaniac). I tried to make her see herself as a selfish prude. Even during my most intense efforts, I don't think I ever fully convinced her to believe these lies. Instead, my plot backfired again because the pressure I put on Patti drove her more and more into the arms of Jesus.

I continued to overreact with Patti just as I had the day she failed to serve potatoes with the evening meal. If she told me I talked too much during a visit to someone's house, I would give myself an order to say almost nothing the next time we were out with friends. If we were riding in the car and she said or acted like I was driving too fast, I would slow the car to an exasperating snail's pace. Whenever she complained about my sermon being too long, the next one wouldn't even qualify as a sermonette. The message was clear. If Patti thought there was anything she should say to me, she would have to pay dearly for the privilege of saying it. I meted out cruel punishment to anyone who dared to speak against "his royal highness."

After I finished seminary and began to work as a pastor, our children came along. Now I had the added responsibility of parenthood, for which I was as ill-prepared as I had been for marriage. But the reality of it wouldn't go away. God was drawing me further into His net, and I was desperately resisting. More than anything I wanted to escape, so much so that I was even willing to look less like a "darn good husband." The facade was beginning to fade and I had less energy than ever to properly maintain it.

Things began to look worse, but the truth was that they were getting better because I was beginning to wear out. The day was much nearer when I would see and confess my utter helplessness, my inability to function successfully as a husband, a parent, a pastor—even as a human being. On that day, I would come to know Jesus as never before.

3

The Pretzel Period

A Backwoods Country Preacher

"Page, you'll never be anything more than a backwoods country preacher!"

My college speech professor said this, and I was fuming. What did he know? Outwardly, I grinned sheepishly—as I was sure that any good-hearted, mature fellow would do under such trying circumstances. His words stung me, and I resented him for years afterward. I promised myself I would prove him wrong. Someday I would pastor one of those prestigious downtown churches in Atlanta, maybe even in Washington, D.C. He'd see! I'd be the next Peter Marshall, and I'd teach him a thing or two.

That is where I usually was in my mind. On top. I was the teacher, not the pupil. I was the physician, not the patient. I was the boss, not the employee. I was the hero, not the villain. It's no wonder my speech professor was finally driven to slap me in the face with those words. I was undoubtedly one of the most stubborn and unteachable students of his career. No one could tell me anything, for I already knew it all.

My first pastorates were among small congregations in Mississippi and Florida. They were a far cry from Atlanta and Washington, D.C., but they were just what I needed. They made me a little frantic because the people treated me like an ordinary person rather than Mr. Wonderful, and I felt uncomfortably close to being a backwoods country preacher in those places. Reality was impinging on my existence with increasing frequency, and I reacted like a pretzel. *I got all bent out of shape!*

Because Patti remained the greatest source of reality in my life, I stayed away from home as much as possible. I did this mostly by getting very busy in the pastorate. Deep down I knew—although I wasn't aware of it at the time—that there was a big hole in my life. I didn't really have what it took, so I redoubled my efforts. Pious religiosity oozed from my pores, but it wouldn't fill that hole.

My real goal was to bring in the kingdom of H. Page Williams, not the Kingdom of God. Of course, I could not do that either, because that is God's job. Therefore, I had to get everybody to like (love, honor, worship and adore) me. So I was always the "nice guy." I would not confront people. I was just agreeable old Rev'run Williams, the most wishy-washy preacher—and person—in town.

A lot of people slapped me on the back and told me what a swell guy I was, but I had almost no friends in those days. Who would have wanted a friend like me? I stood for nothing; I was a giant zero. For that reason, I was an obvious target for every con man in town. I couldn't say no to anyone, for fear that they might not like me. So I worked assiduously to please salesmen, repairmen, freeloaders and all sorts of ne'er-do-wells, while treating my own family like dirt.

I should have been admitted to the mental ward of the local hospital, but instead I was supposedly shepherding a flock of God's sheep. Somehow, those sheep survived my pastorate. After all, by the measurement of the Apostle Paul, since I wasn't doing so well ruling my own family, I was totally unqualified to pastor a church (1 Tim. 3:5). The sheep survived solely on the basis of God's mercy, overcoming the effects of my darkness.

Mixed Signals

I don't want to invade the privacy of the rest of my family, so I won't go into detail as to how my behavior affected my wife and children. Suffice it to say that it was enough to drive anybody crazy. They were getting conflicting signals from me all the time. By my actions and attitudes I was expressing hatred and rejection, while with my lips I was proclaiming my love for them. As someone has said, "Behavior is attitude on display." Actions speak louder than words, but I was yelling pretty loudly. It must have been enormously confusing.

But reality (God) was incessantly battering at the walls of my kingdom—we Presbyterians call it "irresistible grace"—and I was the one who was completely confused. I actually believed that I was a wonderful person in the face of overwhelming evidence to the contrary.

What is remarkable in all this is how stable Patti remained through it. She had been driven into a deeper dependency on God the Father, the Son and the Holy Spirit, and it made a big difference in her ability to cope with me. Pretty steadily she withstood me, telling me the truth when I wanted to believe a lie, and coming back again and again no matter how much I punished her by the emotional pressure I inflicted.

As time went on, I punished Patti more and more severely for her stand with God. Toward the end, I had nearly frozen her out of my life entirely. She and the children might just as well have been a widow and orphans. I buried myself in "church work" more than ever. On my day off I'd be sure to arrange something to keep me out of the house, like a golf outing. I told Patti I had to get out on the golf course to relieve the pressures I was under at church. But that was not altogether true. I was mistaking the pressures at home for the pressures at church, and did not know the difference. I loved the "church work" because it usually pumped up my ego very nicely. I could spend hours on the golf course, but I could not find even a few minutes to fix something or otherwise help around the house.

I really punished Patti when it came to sex. But reality got the best of me in this department rather quickly. With my libido, I could only ignore her for so long. Then I would come on like a wild bull. Needless to say, Patti was seldom thrilled by my advances on these intermittent occasions. So I punished her more with verbal abuse about her being frigid and puritanical. I even clubbed her over the head with my favorite Bible verse for such occasions, "For the wife does not rule over her own body, but the husband does..." (1 Cor. 7:4).

After a while, our conversations amounted to little more than arguments. We disagreed about money, child-rearing, sex, worship, recreation, in-laws—just about everything. Actually, the arguments never amounted to much. I always outwardly acquiesced to Patti's ideas so that I could hold it against her—and maybe even make her feel guilty about "always" getting her way. I also managed to find little ways to sabotage her ideas. Then, when they failed to work out because of my sabotage, it would show how bad her ideas were.

Sabotage can take hundreds of forms. It may mean spending money so that no one can carry out the ideas you disagree with. Or it may mean arranging the details of a family outing so that everyone has a miserable time—if, for example, the outing was your wife's idea in the first place. Ah, the joys of passive-aggressive behavior!

The only solution, humanly speaking, to the mess I had made of our marriage was to end it all with a divorce. The stigma of divorce in our society has diminished in the last forty years. Even clergymen can survive its rigors today and remain clergymen, at least in certain denominations. But the expense is still great, and the humiliation and grief are still immeasurable. So, many couples live together under the terms of an uneasy truce by which they each agree to go their own way and not trouble the other. This was definitely the way I wanted to go. I was too self-righteous to ask Patti for a divorce.

"Living With You Is Like Hell!"

As time went on, I became more and more miserable. My little ploys kept backfiring with greater frequency. Patti was onto my ways and was almost

29

impossible to fool. In the early days of our marriage she had given her allegiance almost entirely to me, but that did not last long. Slowly, God drew her back to himself. Now she was looking to Him for the answers. She knew I didn't have any in spite of all my propaganda to the contrary. It was humiliating. Here I was—in my fantasy and idolatry—the fount of all wisdom and knowledge, and my own wife failed to recognize it. Alas. My anger grew and my depression deepened until I was tormented by it (I had sown torment for a long time; now it was time for me to reap what I had sown).

Finally, one morning as I was getting ready to leave the house for work, I felt like I was going to explode. "Patti, I think I'm going crazy!" I exploded.

"What do you mean, Page?" she asked.

"I don't know. Forget it. Good-bye."

"Bye, bye, honey," she cooed.

But halfway to work, I turned the car around and headed back to the house.

Patti looked surprised. "Home so soon?" she asked as she cupped her hand over the phone.

I ordered her to get off the phone and then commanded, "Sit down, Patti, I want to talk." My voice was not pleasant. "I can't stand it any longer. Living with you is like hell. I hate you and our life together. Everything about it makes me sick!"

God's Spirit was surely with Patti, for instead of overreacting to my cruel comments, she simply said, "Page, just try to be more specific." There was a lot of pain mixed with determination in Patti's voice.

"All right, you asked for it." I proceeded to lash out at her. All the veiled resentments and bitterness I held inside came spewing out unveiled for the first

30

time. I didn't care about being Mr. Nice Guy anymore. All I wanted to do was clobber Patti. But at the same time, I was exposing myself for who I really was. Somehow, by the grace of God, I was letting it out. It was all there—the cruelty, the abuse, the envy, the competition, the vindictiveness, the hypocrisy, the self-righteousness, the hatred.

Of course, Patti was hurting. Tears streamed quietly down her sweet cheeks as one barrage after another came down on her head. But she kept listening and, deep inside, she knew it was the best thing that had happened for our marriage in a long time. The Holy Spirit graced her to bear the pain and find out how He wanted her to respond. So she prayed and sang to herself, "On Christ the solid rock I stand...Lord, lift me up...."

Finally, after quite a while, it was all out. I slumped back in my chair and waited to see what Patti would do or say. I was still angry and wasn't about to listen to any of her religious platitudes. My eyes glared at her.

"Page, are you a Christian?"

I was stunned. Always before, when anyone asked a question like that of me, I was indignant. Of course I was a Christian!

But now, all of a sudden, scenes out of my past showed large on the inner screen of my mind. All those times Patti had asked me if I had been praying about some matter of importance to us, I had not prayed at all. All those times I was supposed to find out the will of God for our family, I had not, in fact, really cared what the will of God was. Now I had to face what my uncaring actually meant.

I began to weep bitterly. It occurred to me that I was a hypocrite, a liar, a false Christian. I had said I was a Christian because of the good feeling I had when I walked down the aisle of the First Baptist Church at the age of nine. But that walk and my baptism had been without repentance; time had amply demonstrated that. I "professed" my faith in Christ, but had not "progressed" in that faith. I had not really seen myself as a sinner in need of forgiveness—until now.

Thus, on that same day, I found myself kneeling beside our bed, hand in hand with Patti, confessing as a sinner my need for Christ. It was wonderful, but within a few days I saw that my heart hadn't changed much. So, back I went to my bedside to ask Jesus again to save me and change my heart. As more time passed, I saw that my heart was still hard. I was the same old Page, selfish to the core. I began to despair, thinking perhaps that I had so twisted my life that it was beyond redemption (these thoughts, I now recognize, were coming straight from my idolatrous nature desperately hoping to make it through this ordeal alive). But I was determined to take hold of Jesus, or maybe more accurately to let Him take hold of me on His terms.

I knelt for a third time to plead for His mercy. As I did, something began to dawn on me. *I, not my parents, my childhood environment, my wife, my job, my friends or the devil—but I alone—was responsible for my predicament.* It began to dawn on me that it was my own choices and decisions that had put me where I was, and this gave me hope. I did not have to depend on others to get me out. All I needed to do was to begin making choices and decisions in accordance with God's Word and will, and then I would gradually begin the upward spiral, rather than stewing in the pit.

As I thought about it, I saw that I had consistently excused my sin by blaming it on others. Now, by the grace of God, I began to be willing to accept the blame myself. I had chosen the kind of life I would live. My responses of anger and self-pity were things I freely selected—nobody made me angry (although that's what we always think, isn't it?). Anger is a natural response in any person, but why? In theological seminary I had learned that our natures are totally corrupted by sin. Now I saw what that meant in more realistic and concrete terms. From childhood I had developed a feeling about myself that was idolatrous; I saw myself as a god-like person, perfect in every way.

It was all right for me to get angry as long as I let it expose my idolatry and self-love in order that I could go to God in search of mercy. But I got off the track when I chose to conceal my anger for the purpose of affirming the image I had created for myself. In so doing, I refused to look at who I *really* was, which meant I was cut off from Christ because He came for sinners, not for self-righteous folks.

Since I was nine years old, I relied on my experience that day in my grandparents' church to authenticate my being a Christian. I wanted to believe that a single magical experience, accompanied preferably by euphoric feelings, would transform me painlessly into a glowing, ready-made saint. I wanted to come to terms with God and be done with Him as quickly as possible so that I could go on living my own way, pleasing myself. I didn't want to be bothered with a day-by-day walk of dependence and obedience.

When Patti asked me if I was saved, it triggered a response that was eventually very positive. Now, if you asked me when I was saved, I couldn't tell you. Bishop Lightfoot was once asked if he was saved, and he replied, "Sir, I have been saved. I am being saved. And I shall be saved." He was a great New Testament student and knew that salvation was not merely an event that occurs at a moment in the past, but, in a much larger sense, it is a *process*. The date of the initiation of my salvation is not the important question—besides, the Bible says I was chosen in Him before the foundation of the world (Eph. 1:4)—but what is important is the extent to which I am walking in the Spirit and light today.

The King Abdicates His Throne

God promises to take away our hearts of stone and give us hearts of flesh. When I began to be willing, in even the smallest way, to be needful of God day after day, my heart began to change. I actually began to want to fellowship with God, the Father, Son and Holy Spirit. I even felt genuinely grateful for His love and mercy. And my compulsive drive to establish my kingdom of self began to diminish little by little. Strangely, the deep inner hunger that seemed insatiable no matter how often my ego was stroked and petted now became less intense as I learned to live in reality as an ordinary person rather than as a god among his servants. What a relief it was to come down off the lofty throne on which I had sat so precariously for so many years. I felt as if I had been released from prison.

That was the critical turning point. It was, as I look back on it now, only a glimmer of light in my dense darkness. At the time it flashed like lightning and gave me hope. I no longer had that trapped feeling that always came when I blamed others for my experiences. Things looked very hopeful indeed because I didn't have to get other people to change in order for me to be at peace or happy. I couldn't change myself either, but I could invite God to change me—in a way I couldn't invite Him to change other people.

Little by little, the Lord started showing me His plan for my marriage, as little by little I was willing to listen. My opinions were shattered one after another. He kept telling me that the way up was the way down, that the way to live was to die, that to get I must give, and that if I wanted to be first, I needed to be last. It seemed like double-talk. Sure, I'd read it all before in the Bible and I knew in my head that these were the paradoxes of the Kingdom of God. But when it got down to the details of my life, I was not all that enthusiastic—in fact, it was very painful.

Take, for example, the way in which I should be a father to my son. I'd always thought that meant that I should take him with me hunting and fishing, like my stepfather did with me—that we should have fun together doing "manly" things. It was not immediately thrilling to me to discover that Jesus was more interested in having Perry see me acting responsibly as a husband and father in the home. This meant treating my wife, his mother, with proper respect and really loving her. It meant doing work around the house with a good attitude, not waiting to be nagged by my wife. It meant helping keep the bathroom and toilet clean, doing laundry, helping make the bed, helping with the grocery shopping and cooking—all that stuff that was "woman's work." Yuck! But I could do it by praying and thanking Jesus for this opportunity to show love, kindness and responsibility to my wife and family.

My opinion about Patti was completely reversed. Where I had seen her as ill-tempered, prudish, scolding and cold, now I perceived her as a warm, loving, caring person. I had wanted flattery, subservience and acquiescence. Now I began to want truth, honesty and the kind of *agape* love the Bible talks about, not the *eros* love the world talks about. In those terms, Patti looked entirely different. She was no longer the shrew and competitor I had made her out to be; now she was the "model" wife.

The key to this change in my attitude was simple. As long as I was caught in my idolatry so that I took myself seriously as a godlike person among his servants, then other people could never be my equal. But once I began to let Jesus be my Lord, then I was down on the same level with all the rest of the folks. On that level, I could begin to regard Patti as a person rather than as a housekeeper and sex object. That means I can appreciate her anger as well as her softness, her saltiness as well as her sweetness; she expresses both at different times according to the occasion. God has given me a wonderful gift— a wife who loves Jesus.

One way in which I've begun to cherish her is to consistently see to it that we have some private time in order to get away from the demands of the ministry. We're not legalistic about this, but I really do want to be sensitive to the Holy Spirit who teaches me how to really love my wife.

One morning I woke up around 4:30 and found Patti awake, too. "What are you doing, honey?" I asked.

"I'm praying."

"That's great! You know what? I think I will go into the kitchen and fix us a little something to eat. I think it would be nice."

36

"Oh, Page, you shouldn't bother. Why don't you just get back to sleep? You need your rest."

"No, Patti, I really want to do it. You just wait here."

A few minutes later I was back from the kitchen with fresh cups of coffee and some toast and jelly. We sat up in the bed and ate and talked and giggled for nearly two hours. It was a time of intimacy and refreshment for both of us.

On another occasion, I received a phone call from a church inviting Patti and I to put on a weekend family life conference for them. It was less than a day's drive from us and I told them we'd be there. But when I told Patti about it, she immediately popped out with her feelings. "No! I don't want to go!"

"But why not, honey?" I asked. I was a bit taken back.

"Well, I don't know, but I'll pray about it."

I decided I'd better pray about it, too. And when I did, I realized that my motives for accepting the invitation were not entirely pure and that it did not fit very well into our schedule. I went back to Patti and told her that I had prayed about the situation and that I would call the church and get out of doing the conference. She was surprised and delighted, and I was thankful for an honest wife. If we had gone to that conference without the blessing and direction of God, it would have been disastrous.

One day, when our daughter Plythe was about thirteen, I asked her, without any warning, "What are you feeling?"

"I don't know, daddy. What am I supposed to be feeling?"

I could see that she was indeed my daughter. Like me, she was hiding from her own feelings because she thought it was more important to win other people's approval, especially her father's.

"Sweetheart," I said, "you're not *supposed* to be feeling anything. It is just that we all have feelings and thoughts all the time, and I was just interested to know what was going on inside you."

Plythe was convinced that I would like her better if she just kept her emotions to herself and tried her best to be a sweet little daddy's girl. So, that day I didn't learn much about how she felt, even about the weather. But, the day did come, after Plythe had watched her mom speak her mind and heart to me several times without getting her head bitten off for it, that she decided to give it a try. It happened on a very safe occasion, when Patti and I were hugging, that Plythe came up and announced, "I'm jealous." Patti and I were both delighted, and we immediately included her in our hugging while our poodle danced around our heels, trying to get into the circle of affection, too.

There was a time when I was so idolatrous that I was actually afraid to say no to my children. I wanted them to like me so much that I abandoned my protective responsibility toward them. It was a sick situation, and I was well on the way toward raising two idolaters like myself. But, in more recent years, thank God, I've learned to say no and to care deeply about my children and the kind of people they are. I know many psychologists would say that it's too late—because after the first five years of life, personality patterns are set and that's that. I don't quarrel with them except to say that our God is a God of miracles. He made the blind see, the deaf hear and the likes of me to grow up and accept responsibility.

With God, our children can also change.

So, we try to introduce our children to our heavenly Father as the One on whom they must rely throughout life. We teach them what He has promised and what He expects from us. If they learn to know God personally, they'll be ready when the time comes for them to leave the nest and start out on their own. We will not always be there to help them, so we are teaching them to depend less on us and more on God. For example, if a child comes home complaining that some bully threw rocks at him after school, instead of spending our time lamenting about how bad that bully was and how mean it was of him to throw rocks, we might start off by asking the child to ask Jesus to show him why He let that happen. This sometimes brings hidden sin to the surface where it can be dealt with through confession and repentance. Later, after the child has gotten the benefit of the experience, we might call the school to quietly bring the incident to the attention of the proper authorities.

In the Bible, James begins his epistle by writing that we should count it all joy when we encounter various trials because they produce endurance in us. He goes on to explain, "But let the process go on until that endurance is fully developed, and you will find that you have become men of mature character with the right sort of independence" (James 1:4, Phillips). We have found that when we don't try to excessively protect our children from the tribulations of growing up, but instead let those experiences bring them to Jesus, it happens exactly as James says. They develop the right sort of independence—God dependence and interdependence.

Plythe once decided to try out to become a majorette at her junior high school. Both Patti and I wondered how she would take it if she didn't make it. The competition was stiff. One evening Patti and I were talking with Plythe about it.

"Plythe," Patti began, "you know how we've encouraged you to get your real feelings out with us. Well, you should do that with God, too. Tell Him how you feel about this majorette competition—how much you want to win and how afraid you are to lose. And you can ask Him to help you win, if you want. There's nothing wrong with that."

"That's right, Plythe," I joined in. "God's the only one who knows for sure what will happen. Your mom and I sure don't, and we're probably as nervous as you are. But we do know that God loves you and that whatever happens will be in His hands and turn out for the best. If you lose, He'll show you why and you'll get a great blessing. If you win, He'll give you the grace to handle the success without thinking it makes you better than anyone else. Just get your feelings out and then ask Him to help you accept His decision."

Plythe listened to us that night, and I think it put her a step closer to Jesus. As it turned out, God gave her the harder test. She made the squad!

Plythe had gotten to know the Lord better on a previous occasion through her experience in wanting a horse. For two years she prayed for a horse of her own. At first, she prayed for a horse to ride and "show" and enjoy. But, as the Holy Spirit gently taught her, she began to pray for a horse to care for and enjoy. Thereupon her prayers shone brighter with faith, and within a short time, God had worked out the details and Plythe had her horse. But He knew she wasn't ready to withstand the temptation to self-importance that any child would experience astride a horse in front of other children. So, He gave her a horse that was a carrier of a disease called "swamp fever." As a result, she couldn't show off that horse, but it was able to be stabled within walking distance of our home and in an area where she could ride to her heart's content. I often heard her exclaim how happy she was that God gave her a horse to love and enjoy.

Sometimes, when I get to thinking about all that God has done for me and my family, I realize I could never thank Him sufficiently for it all. I often ask, "Lord, how can I thank you more fully for your grace and mercy to a person as undeserving as I am?"

His answer to me has been straightforward and simple, "Page, keep laughing at yourself and taking Me seriously. Do what I tell you and enjoy what I give you." Amen.

41

4

Getting Into It

One evening when Patti and I were out at a meeting, our teen-aged son Perry answered the phone.

"Hello."

"Is this the H. Page Williams' residence?" It was a woman's voice.

"Yes, but my parents aren't home just now," Perry responded. "May I take a message?"

"Yes, you can. I was recently divorced. It was terrible, and I was becoming very depressed. My husband blamed me for everything that had gone wrong. When we finally parted, I felt utterly worthless. My life wasn't worth living.

"So, I got a prescription for sleeping pills, intending to use them to end it all. I got to the pharmacy and was waiting for the prescription to be filled when I saw your father's book, *Do Yourself a Favor: Love Your Wife*, on the book rack. I picked it up and started reading. I became so fascinated by what it said that I forgot the prescription, bought the book instead and took it home to finish.

"When I saw that other husbands treated their wives the same way mine had treated me, I began to realize that it was not all my fault. It gave me hope. I know God sent that book to me. So, tell your father his book didn't save my marriage, but it did save my life!"

She exaggerated. My book didn't save her life; God did. But I was thrilled to see how the Holy Spirit used the book to help a woman. I wrote it to men and for men. But God is never limited by our narrow perspectives.

Most often, the book has stirred people up enough to get them to come out in the open so that they can get some help. I remember receiving a phone call one time from a man in Oregon. He was very upset.

"Mr. Williams, you don't know me, but I read your book, and I want to know what you think about my situation. My wife sleeps in the bedroom, but I sleep on the couch. It's been that way for months now. You see it's her parents. They hate me, and the feeling is mutual. They're Mormons and I'm a Catholic. They say that if I loved their daughter, I'd become a Mormon, and I insist that she ought to join me as a Catholic.

"My wife doesn't want any more children—we have three—because she doesn't think we can afford them. She always says we don't have enough money. Whenever I have a few days off and suggest that we get away from the house, all she ever wants to do is go see her folks. I hate that. I'd rather get out and see some sights or do some camping—"

I was amazed. In a few sentences this man—his name was John—had touched upon every major area of conflict that most couples experience: sex, in-laws,

44

religion, communication, children, money and recreation. As I listened to him, I knew it would take nothing short of a miracle to save his marriage. Unsure as to where to begin, I shot up a prayer and then launched in.

"John, your problems come from you and your wife's selfishness and immaturity. You have to look at your sin, humble yourself, repent and pray. No one but God can help you, and the help you get will have to be on His terms."

I believe John heard what I was saying and I know that God's Word always accomplishes its purpose. I prayed for him on the phone that he would become desperate enough to trust in God's way.

Marriage Means Conflict

Marriage means conflict. It couldn't mean anything else in a sinful world. Different groups of people handle it in different ways, but in America today the overwhelming first choice is to resolve the conflicts by divorce. Even marriages that don't end in divorce do not necessarily represent happy unions of mature, wonderful people either. In many cases, they represent real horror stories of women giving up their very personhoods to become sex objects and housekeepers. There are books—some of them have sold in the millions—that tell women just how to do it and try to convince them that they will like it.

God hates divorce, and He abhors oppression. Neither one gets to the heart of the problem—human selfishness. Only God's grace can penetrate that barrier and bring the salvation that was purchased by the blood of Jesus.

45

In *Do Yourself a Favor: Love your Wife,* I talked about how we need to see our own faults, not those of others, in our marriage problems. Saving our homes is a possibility within our grasp, *if* we are willing to obey God.

I remember the first time I visited the home of one of my parishioners. His name was Tom Jackson, and he was a successful farmer with a lovely home. I noticed a stack of manuals beside his big easy chair. They looked like they had been thumbed through many times.

"Tom," I asked, "do you really read all those manuals?"

"Yes I do, pastor. I believe in using the best and most up-to-date tools available to do a job. So I buy a lot of equipment, and each piece is usually accompanied by a manual. Regardless of how much I may think I know about that new piece of machinery, I always take time to read that manual. Farm equipment costs a lot of money, and I do myself a favor by finding out how to take care of it and what it can do for me."

I knew I had met a wise man. Tom was now past retirement age and going strong. He was not in debt. His home was in a beautiful setting between two lakes. Live oaks and pecan trees provided a shady haven of the property around his house. The key to his success obviously had something to do with his teachableness and lack of arrogance. Those qualities were not limited to his farming either, but seemed to stretch over his entire life. Right beside that stack of farm machinery manuals was a *Living Bible* and a copy of *Do Yourself a Favor: Love Your Wife.* Tom evidently felt the same way about his soul and his wife as he did about his farm equipment.

That made me very happy. In writing *Do Your-self a Favor: Love Your Wife*, I intended for it to be a manual for men who want to become what God wants them to be and to learn how to properly care for their wives.

I can't pass by the story of Tom Jackson without telling a little story about my wife Patti, which she has given me permission to tell. On one of her first visits to the Jackson home, Tom rode up to the house to greet her in a new, air-conditioned combine. He got out and was telling her what the machine could do. Then he asked her, "How much do you think one of these combines costs?"

"I don't have any idea, Tom," Patti responded.

"Would you believe $26,000.00?" (A lot of money in those days.)

Patti was flabbergasted. That night, as she told the rest of us about her visit, she said, "And guess what Tom Jackson pays for his concubines?" My jaw fell, but she didn't even notice that she had used the biblical word for mistress. She announced, "$26,000.00!"

"Wow," I gasped, "that's a mighty high price for a mistress!"

Patti "got it," and blushed as the rest of us guffawed. Our teen-age son Perry couldn't pass up an opportunity like this, either, "But, mom, I always thought Tom Jackson was a nice man."

Here's a letter that especially thrilled me:

Dear Sir:

No self-respecting male would dare read a book like *Do Yourself A Favor: Love Your Wife*, especially if his wife suggested it. I was fortunate,

47

though, because my daughter gave me a copy for Father's Day. She had attended a series of lectures on marriage at her college and your book was recommended reading. It gathered dust on a shelf for a while, but one day I picked it up— and I couldn't put it down! What a book—what insight! It's all there and more. It's up to me now.

I am grateful for this turn of events and especially to you for writing such an inspiring book— one which I thought I didn't need. I'll give you and the Holy Spirit credit.

Thanks so much.

How God pours out His mercy on us! Here a stubborn, selfish and egotistical man—like you and me—*changed his mind.* By saying, "It's up to me now," he assumed the responsibility to solve his homemade problems. He stepped into line as the head of his wife, under the headship of Christ.

It almost invariably happens that once Christ really has a hold on a person, that person's life becomes outwardly worse before it becomes better. That is because the Holy Spirit is free to start dredging up a person's sin. Once out in the open, sin loses its power. It needs to be confessed. This is the basic process of salvation, and it can be quite painful at times. But God is in control and will bring it to a good end.

Perhaps this letter will illustrate what I mean:

Dear Pastor Williams,

Since reading *Do Yourself a Favor: Love Your Wife,* I see more clearly that I am a givingless person. I created the problems of my marriage with my own insecurity and self-centeredness....

48

I have been married four years. My wife has tried to tell me that the way I am only drives us apart. I felt remorseful when she told me these things, but I never did anything about it. Only when things got really bad did I try to find out why I acted that way. So I began to blame my childhood, my parents and my early environment. Carole and I talked about these things endlessly, but it didn't help much. Finally I began to pray for guidance and forgiveness. I was beginning to be really desperate.

That's about the time I found and bought your book. It was the first thing I had read about marriage that made any sense. I was on every page of that book. It was uncanny. I've taken what you said and made it a standard to live by.

Now I've turned completely around. I can't give enough. In fact, I think I've gone overboard. Carole says I smother her and no matter how much I explain my new attitudes to her, she remains skeptical. It seems like I can't do anything right. Sometimes I'm more frustrated that ever. A lot of times Carole doesn't want to have anything to do with me, and I have to pray for patience. It's hard.

Maybe I've gone beyond forgiveness for the way I've treated her these last four years. I hate to think of how I was, and I marvel to think how steadily Carole tried to make me see who l was and what I was doing. It makes me love her more deeply than ever. When I feel that happening, I have hope for the future.

This is a classic case. The author of this letter has seen his sin, but instead of simply repenting and asking Jesus to change his heart, he tried to atone for it himself by reversing his behavior. This showed up when his wife complained that he was smothering her. To correct that, he'll have to go back to Jesus. The more secure a man becomes in his relationship with Christ, the more he releases his wife from the pressure of having to hold him up. A secure relationship with God means faith. So, the problem is unbelief. The solution is to confess that unbelief and ask for forgiveness, and ask Jesus to change your heart. We don't really believe that Jesus' blood is sufficient for our sins, even though we say we do.

When a man is in this process of confession and cleansing, he is loving the Lord. His wife will feel protected, in turn, because God does protect those who fear Him—and their households. And a wife who feels protected is a responsive wife. She is free to respond because she is not uptight and doesn't have to worry about protecting herself.

I am not talking about a man acting in a super-spiritual way. That is fanaticism which seeks to avoid the way of the cross and fly up to high places on one's own wings. It's a spiritual ego trip. You can easily spot a person who is being super-spiritual. Anytime you're around him, you get the idea that you should feel very inferior because he's so spiritual.

What I am talking about is a husband who talks sanely with his heavenly Father about every matter and detail of his life. He is consistently dependent on God for wisdom and insight in every situation as it arises. He doesn't trust himself or his knowledge. He regularly consults the manual—the Bible—in an effort to listen to God and become better acquainted with Him. He knows that he is a sinner and he is not surprised to find it in himself. Instead he confesses it and asks for mercy daily (Col. 2:6) without feeling sorry for himself.

This brings us to the next chapter, where we'll look at the basic steps a man must take to start *thinking* like a godly husband.

5

How to Think Like a Godly Husband

One evening, as Patti and I were working in the kitchen, the phone rang. "Hello, Page Williams speaking."

"Yes, this is Bill Boggs. You don't know me, but I surely do know you."

"How is that?" I asked.

"My wife literally hit me over the head with your book and dared me to read it. Well, I stayed up half the night to finish it once I got started. Hey, boy, I'm going to have to come down there and talk to you about this stuff."

When a Southerner calls me boy, I know I'm in trouble! He was obviously ruffled. I don't like to schedule appointments with angry men, but he was persistent, and I felt the Lord tell me to go ahead. I asked God to protect me, and we lined up a time for him to come for a visit.

He was a medical doctor and sounded large and imposing on the phone. It turned out that he was a bit shorter than I, so I felt less intimidated after he arrived. We spent most of the day trying to convince him that he was rebelling against God, not me. But he was sure the problems in his marriage were the fault of his wife and her parents. Patti and I tried to help him see his arrogance and rebellion, but he insisted it couldn't be true because he had been baptized in the Holy Spirit and was the most Spirit-filled man in his area.

"My trouble is," he insisted, "I'm just *too* good."

This was interesting, so I suggested, "Tell me about it."

"My wife fusses at me because I buy these Christian books to give away to folks and because I go to Christian conferences all over the country. Now what is wrong with that?"

But, before I could say a word, he began dropping names of all the religious leaders he had personally talked with. Then he started telling us about his various good deeds and how helpful he was to all the widows and divorcees. This sounded a little suspicious, but as I had prayed, I felt a nudge from the Holy Spirit that I needed to follow up on first.

"Bill," I interrupted, "do you pay your bills?"

He looked stricken for a moment, but he then began to carry on as before, "That's another thing my wife doesn't understand. Just because she gets a few calls from creditors about late bills, she gets angry."

The more he talked, the sicker we got. Bill had obviously not come to hear any counsel. He just wanted a name to add to his list of important people with whom he had talked. From that remark about the widows and divorcees, we also began to suspect that much of his religious intensity was just a cover-up for sexual adventures.

We continued seeing Bill occasionally during the next few months, and it finally all came out in the

54

open. His wife learned of his exploits from a couple of those widows and divorcees he had been "helping." But Bill would never own up to it. He resolutely insisted that he was a good and righteous man, and his marriage failed because of his wife. The court battle was an ugly affair that left scars on the whole family and community.

I'd like to contrast the story of Bill Boggs with that of Mike Jordon. This contrast shows, among other things, that the enormity of one's sins does not necessarily determine the outcome of a marital conflict.

Mike was a big man. He was a football player in college and later married into a wealthy family. He was afraid that people might think he lived off his wife's wealth (which is another way of saying he had some ego problems), so he set out to prove that wasn't true. He got in with a land development firm that started making money hand over fist. Success bred arrogance in the firm's partners. These men were riding high. After a while, a few shady deals and a little income tax fraud didn't trouble them at all. Mike joined right in. He deducted the expenses of his racing cars from his income tax and began enjoying the company of women who were as fast as the cars.

While Mike lived out his fantasies away from home, he was careful to maintain a facade of respectability. He and his wife were active church members and Sunday school teachers. They had six children. However, the happy picture was marred by the death of one of the children. The child, seven years of age, tried to ride one of the ponies on the ranch, with disastrous results. Mike wasn't ready to ask himself why such a thing had happened. It hardly dented his self-sufficiency, and whatever pain he felt, he tried to bury in a flurry of activity.

Inflation began to rise in our country in the early seventies. Mike's investments were obliterated, and he ended up in bankruptcy. God was really tightening the circle of His love around Mike now, and Mike ran more scared than ever. In deep self-pity, he rationalized his way through a whole parcel of affairs, washing down any signs of a troubled conscience with liberal doses of alcohol.

He continued trying to keep up his facade as a good guy at home, but it didn't work. His double life finally short-circuited, and his wife threw him out of the house. Mike slunk away to a little apartment to nurse his wounds. But his disastrous decline awakened him, because when a friend gave him a copy of *Do Yourself a Favor: Love your Wife*, he actually read it—in one night. The Holy Spirit spoke to him that night, and with God's help, he was able to hear. The following evening he attended a Methodist Church. At the end of the service he walked down the aisle to the front of the sanctuary to give his life to Christ. His heart was broken and his spirit was contrite.

The first thing he wanted to do was to get honest with his wife. He called her, and although she had already instituted divorce proceedings, God helped her to be willing to see him just one more time. They talked that night in a quiet, out-of-the-way restaurant. Mike was talking straight for the first time in years. He told his wife Mary about his inner feelings, his sins, his crazy notions—everything. Gone was the arrogance, the pride, the self-sufficiency and the ugliness that had destroyed their marriage. In its place was a lowly man who seemed to genuinely respect the woman with whom he was talking. Mary felt it all and began to soften. They agreed to seek counsel together and to see if God could work a miracle in their marriage and their lives.

It was just a day or so later that Patti answered the phone and first heard Mike Jordon's voice. He and Mary wanted to fly across the country to see us and talk about how to get their marriage in order. When they arrived, Mike was a humbled man, ready to listen. With relatively little struggle, we were able to help them see what God was asking of them. Today, Mike and Mary and their children are walking together on a rough but radiant road of trust in the Lord.

Recognize Your Need

Now on to the topic of this chapter. To begin to *think* like a godly husband, you must have the *desire* to be a godly husband. In fact, you have to want it so much that you "hunger and thirst" for it. That means recognizing your need. There are three kinds of people in the world: (1) those who think they have no needs, (2) those who know they have needs but are trying to have them met by the world, the flesh or the devil and (3) those who know they have needs and are trusting them with God to be met.

Jesus characterizes these three groups, respectively, with the words "lukewarm" (no needs), "cold" (needs to be met by the world) and "hot" (needs to be met by God), in Revelation 3:15-22. If you are lukewarm, ask Jesus to show you the truth, that you are wretched, pitiable, poor, blind and naked. If you are cold, you are a step closer to God's Kingdom because you are probably stuck in some obvious sin, like drunkenness, immorality, gluttony or compulsive behavior such as gambling. Just ask Jesus to dry up your water hole, unless He already has, and you're ready to repent now.

Honest With God

The second step toward beginning to think like a godly husband is to set your will to keep being honest with God. Once God pulls us out of a bad spot, our tendency is to thank Him politely and resume living according to our own insights and strengths as soon as possible. This usually means that God will have to turn on the pressure again so that we'll come running back. To avoid the pain of crisis after crisis, just settle it in your mind now that you are a needful person and you will be for the rest of your life.

With that settled, you'll be ready to keep up a daily—even hourly—habit of living in the light. This means letting the light of God's Word shine into your life through the Bible, through every experience you have and especially through what other people say to you. That light will expose sin; it will arouse regrets, hatred, resentment, suspicion, fear, anxiety and a host of other negative emotions. Look at them, confess them, thank Jesus for washing you in His blood and ask Him to change your heart.

This is a painful process, and because of that, many men try to avoid it by saying that their problems are beyond solution and that there is nothing left to do but to get a divorce. The man who says that is a liar, and is accusing God of lying. "God...will never let you be tempted beyond what you can stand, but, when temptation comes, he will provide the way out of it, so that you can bear up under it" (1 Cor. 10:13, Moffatt).

God's Economy

The third step toward beginning to think like a godly husband is realizing that God adds to and multiplies whatever you give to Him, and whatever you withhold from Him, He subtracts from and divides. So if you invest none of your time, energy or money in the Kingdom of God, then you have only zero by which to multiply all that God has to give you. And that always amounts to nothing. But if you renounce your rebellion and unbelief, and set yourself toward God to become His servant, then God pours out overflowing blessings both spiritual and material.

Ben and Frances came for counseling one evening. After hearing all the built-up hostilities, let down hopes and hopped-up promises that had buffeted their marriage for years, I wouldn't have given you two cents for it. For a while it seemed as if Ben had convinced himself, Frances, Patti and me that it was all Frances' fault. She acted like she was ready for the state mental hospital. Defeated, rejected and dejected, she was almost incapable of making a sensible decision. But God gave us grace to persist in the face of all the evidence. We focused our attention on Ben, speaking to him of the basics—repentance and faith in the Lord Jesus Christ. That night, in the privacy of his bedroom, he told Jesus that he was a needy sinner, thanked Him for dying on the cross, asked His forgiveness and invited Him to take over his life and change his heart.

God answered that prayer in a marvelous way. As Ben persevered in his commitment to Christ, Frances underwent a most remarkable recovery. The subtle, but enormous, pressures Ben had been putting on her began to be relieved as soon as Ben placed himself in line beneath the Lord. Ben had invested what he had—like I said, I wouldn't have given you two cents for it myself—and God multiplied it so that Ben today has a valuable marriage over which God has set him as a trustee, not an owner.

The most notable change in Ben was that when he was faced with the need to make decisions, instead of "thinking about it"—a process that inevitably produced negative attitudes toward his wife and family—Ben began to ask God to show him what to do. That, in turn, allowed Frances to open up about her feelings. As you might suspect, this meant that things really started to look bad. The Holy Spirit began dredging the repressed resentments of years to the surface. Ben did not know how to deal with a wife who was saying exactly what she thought and felt, but he kept on trusting the Lord. Day by day, God gave them grace and wisdom to work through the conflicts they had with regard to in-laws, sex, finances, vacations, work, children, recreation, church and so on. Whenever they reached an impasse, they would call us, and we would get together. After a while, the snags became fewer and further between. Today, Ben and Frances have learned the rudiments of living in the light, and they're enjoying the consequent benefits.

Run with the Vision

The fourth step toward beginning to think like a godly husband is learning to picture what you want. A man who cannot picture what he wants in his marriage wouldn't know it if he got it. A man with nothing to work toward usually ends up with nothing.

When I counsel couples who are preparing for marriage, I usually ask the prospective groom, "What are you looking for in this marriage?" Most of the time, I get a bewildered stare in response which tells me he hasn't done much thinking about the question—because he really doesn't want to. That is usually because he's ashamed of the answer. Men are usually looking for a lot of sex in marriage. In addition, they like the idea of an unsalaried housekeeper and someone who can take care of them, like their mother used to take care of them.

Needless to say, these are not very admirable goals and aspirations. They represent our self-centeredness. The thing to do is admit it and ask for God's mercy and a change of heart so that you can want and embrace God's vision for your marriage.

Many married men with whom I have talked see marriage as a "50-50" proposition in which responsibility is shared so that it's nobody's fault if it doesn't work out. They also tend to believe that the discipline, spiritual guidance, social development and education of the children is the wife's responsibility.

But, in fact, marriage requires a 100-percent commitment of each participant. A husband is totally responsible for his wife. He must choose to share his life with her in complete honesty and expect the same from her. He must fully want her to be a *person*. He must protect her from harassment and intimidation as well as physical harm.

The Bible contains much that will help us see God's vision for our marriages. I wrote much of *Do Yourself a Favor: Love Your Wife* with the same idea in mind. We need to admit that our own picture, no matter how prettily we paint it, is vile. Then we can ask

God for His vision in its precise terms for our particular marriage.

One Step at a Time

The fifth step toward beginning to think like a godly husband is learning to take only one step at a time. This is another aspect of lowliness. Dwight Eisenhower once said that no matter how famous or great a man becomes, he still must pull on his trousers one leg at a time. Because of our desire to be God, we want to know the future with certainty. And we want to get to the end without going through the means (this, by the way, was Wesley's definition of fanaticism)—we refuse to believe that the way out is the way through because that involves hard work or suffering, things which too many of us regard as synonymous.

God promised Joshua, "Every place that the sole of your foot shall tread upon, that have I given to you..."(Josh. 1:3). Joshua was a valiant and faithful man. God told him that all the district of Canaan was his and urged him to go in and take it. But it didn't happen all at once. One day at a time, Joshua faced one impossible situation after another. Each time, as he depended on God, he found the way to victory. By the time of his death, most, but not all, of the Promised Land was in the possession of the Israelites. Jerusalem, for example, did not fall under their dominion until the time of David.

Jesus told us to pray for our daily bread. If it costs us, on an average, 40 dollars a day to live, we would like God to hand us 1,200 dollars on the first of the month. But He hardly ever does. He supplies our needs as they arise and usually not too far in advance.

As an elderly missionary once put it, "God is never in a hurry, but He is never late either." Let's face it, if He gave us a million dollars, He wouldn't see hide nor hair of us until it was all spent. One step at a time is the way of humility and blessing.

Don't Look Back

The sixth step toward beginning to think like a godly husband is learning to refuse to stop and look back. After we have taken a few steps toward the vision of marriage that God gave us, there is a strong temptation to stop and rest on our laurels. This is very dangerous. Because of who we are (idolaters of ourselves), we inevitably look back at where we've come from only to get proud about it. But this swelling of the ego produces a tidal wave that will bash in the side of the ship of matrimony. If that happens, you'll be back to where you started, or worse.

I remember a young couple my wife and I worked with for about six months. They were doing beautifully. The husband was learning to be honest about his feelings with his wife, and she was seeing who he really was for the first time in their six years of marriage. But then he stopped to look back, as he considered his progress, and he began to rebuild the image of himself as a god. Thereafter, whenever his wife suggested that they pray about whatever was troubling them at the moment, he would refuse. If she complained, he would say, "Well, at least I'm honest." What he didn't realize was that his progress resembled rowing upstream. When he stopped, he immediately began to drift downstream. As I recall, he finally woke up to reality after he crashed over a little

63

waterfall. Then he had to rebuild the boat and start over. It was hard, but God helped him.

Who You Are in Christ and Who He is in You

The seventh and final step toward beginning to think like a godly husband is learning to expand your consciousness of your wealth in Christ and the wife He has given you. Most of us are so absorbed in contemplating the glory of our own navels that we fail to see all that God has given us. Or, if we see it, we despise it because it does nothing to enhance the kingdom of self. Like Esau, we are willing to throw away our inheritance for a bowl of pottage.

What we need is a glad and grateful heart, something that doesn't come naturally. Once again, we need to ask Jesus to help us value the things He values and to be intolerant of the things He doesn't value. This will cut very deeply into the heart of our idolatry, but it is the death that leads to abundant life.

As your God-consciousness expands, you open the gates of your soul for the grace of God to flow in. This fills your inner reservoir with His assets which enable you, in turn, to give love to your wife and family. That is why God-consciousness must always precede wife-consciousness. Unless our love for our wives comes from God, it will necessarily be idolatrous. (By that I mean a contract in which you agree to worship your wife as long as she worships you.)

But once God expands a man from the inside, the man will begin to love, honor and cherish his wife truly. The more a man gets to know God, the more zealous he becomes to fulfill his vows of matrimony—sacred vows. Wedlock really only becomes holy when the husband is wholly surrendered

64

to God and walking humbly with Him.

These seven steps encompass a lifetime. They are not a list to be ticked off smugly by the self-righteous, nor should they be regarded as impossible by the faint of heart. They represent God's principles—things which the Holy Spirit will teach us time and again at every level of life. They can never be left behind, but they can be built upon. In fact, they provide the only solid foundation for marriage because they continually bring us back to Christ as needy sinners.

In the next chapter, I want to examine one of the worst cancers that eat at our marriages. It is as deadly as anything I know of in any relationship, but especially between a husband and wife.

6

Rivalry or Revival?

Competition

How can you add zip and zest to your marriage? I have met very few married people who haven't complained that the intensity of their first love for one another diminished gradually after their wedding. We'll look at why that is and what can be done about it.

There are six ingredients a husband can offer his wife that will really spice up their relationship and cause their love for one another to grow—praise, inspiration, understanding, consideration, service and forgiveness. These are, in fact, expressions of love—not momentary affection, but enduring love. And the major obstacle to their expression is *competition*. Do you perceive your wife as a "competitor" or as a "companion"? Don't answer that question too quickly, at least not before you read the rest of this chapter.

Have you ever told your wife, "There are many fine women in the world, but you surpass them all"? (Prov. 31:29, paraphrased). Patti and I were in a Sunday school group one time in which we were all discussing a certain upcoming project. Various ideas had been put forward and, quite unexpectedly, one man remarked, "I believe my wife's idea was the best!" I glanced at his wife. She was aglow with appreciation. Her husband had praised her in public, without flattery. How unlike the customary way we often make our wives the butts of our jokes, both in their presence and behind their backs.

If a man regards his wife as a competitor, he'll want to keep her down in second place, or in "her place." Thus, the jokes which "put her down" come forth. But if a man is not busy establishing the kingdom of his own frail ego, he will be free to regard his wife not as a threat to his status, but as a companion and lover.

Can you imagine yourself saying the following things in the office or the shop? "My wife's the greatest." "My wife and I had more fun the other night." "Did I tell you about the casserole my wife fixed for supper the other night? It was terrific!" "My wife is a tremendous bookkeeper; if it weren't for her, I'd probably be in jail." "I think my wife's a beautiful woman. She knows how to dress, and she always looks good." If you can't imagine yourself saying these kind of things when they are true, or if you are aware that you don't say them at work or on social occasions, it ought to tell you something about yourself—about your heart attitude. You probably think of your wife as a rival or a threat. Other women can quickly pick up on an attitude like this—just as your wife can. Many of them will correctly interpret it— and the flirtation that often accompanies it—as an invitation from you to move in and take over, because in your heart you've already thrown your wife out. A moment's sober reflection would tell any of us that the sort of woman who would move in at a time like that would be no improvement.

So, ask Jesus to change your heart and teach you how to start praising your wife. Nothing will buoy a discouraged wife's morale like some sincere compliments at the right times.

Another way to check yourself out on this matter is to look at the way your children treat your wife. If youngsters detect a bad attitude in their father toward their mother—and they will, if it's there—they will feel free to turn on her as well, for they now have nothing to fear from dad. How well I remember the evening at our dinner table when Patti was talking to our son Perry about his job. She was pointing out some areas in which he needed to mature, some attitudes that he needed to change. Perry was not thrilled by the lecture and, after a while, pushed his plate of food away and said, "Mom, when you talk to me like this, I can't eat."

Patti fell for it and, while she apologized for upsetting our son, I said nothing. I should have told Perry that he was blaming his mother for his loss of appetite (if, indeed, there was any loss of appetite—he had overloaded his plate in the first place) because he wanted to get even with her for pointing out some areas of weakness. I had to blame myself more than Perry. After all, it was the kind of thing I had pulled on Patti for years; so naturally, our son had learned it from me. And, worse, my silence showed me that my heart hadn't changed as much as I would like to have thought.

The power of praise in a marriage is immeasurable. It encourages and lifts a wife to the extent that she can perform to the fullest those things which God has called her to do. And it is a gift every husband can afford to give when his heart is right.

Inspiration

Closely related to praise is *inspiration*. Do you inspire your wife to do her best by your lively and spirited example? Or do you tend to discourage her? When she has an idea, do you tell her why it's impossible? When she wants to buy something, do you inevitably tell her there's not enough money or make fun of her for "always" wanting to buy something?

Again, if you think of your wife—even subconsciously—as a rival whom you must defeat, it will be impossible for you to inspire her to live up to her full potential. Why should she? She knows that, no matter how hard she tries, you'll only put her down, fearful that she might upstage you.

It's not hard to discover whether or not you're an inspiring husband and father. Just take a good look at your wife and kids. Do they act inspired? Are their lives fruitful? Are they enjoying life to its fullest—or at all? Be a little hard on yourself. For most of us, the word "inspire" doesn't have much positive meaning. It's bland. An inspirational book is usually a bubbly little thing without much substance. But just because we have devalued the word doesn't mean the reality of which it once spoke is any less vital. To inspire is to bring life—abundantly and vibrantly. Without inspiration there will be death.

The need for inspiration takes us right back to Jesus. We can't manufacture inspiration. Instead it comes by the Holy Spirit, who bestows it upon those who humbly recognize and admit that they don't have it to give and are willing to ask for it.

Understanding

Next we'll examine what it means to give *under-standing* to your wife. For years my wife said to me, "You just don't understand." I couldn't understand why she kept saying that because I was sure that I did understand. Now, at this stage in our marriage, I understand what she meant, and she was right. I didn't understand what God wanted of me as the spiritual leader of the home.

One day her words finally struck home. "Page, it's not what I want you to do, but what God wants you to do. That's what I'm talking about." Before then, whenever she told me what to think, where to go or what to do, I simply ignored her because I thought she was being pushy. It never occurred to me that God might speak to me through her. Besides, I couldn't allow that to happen. If it did, it would mean that she was on top and I was on the bottom (because I saw everything in terms of competition instead of companionship).

Now I understand that God gave me my wife as a helper who fits my needs (that's what helpmate means). She is supposed to help me think straight and walk uprightly. She is supposed to offer suggestions and argue with me, to caress and correct me. We like to remember that the Bible refers to our wives as the weaker vessels, but we seldom link that with the Bible's assertion that God chooses what is weak in the world to shame the strong (1 Peter 3:7; 1 Cor. 1:27). In fact, that is a little stronger than I would like to put it, but there it is.

I have been known to really enjoy griping and grumbling about things. But Patti had the habit of letting me know that if I am going to complain about something, it would be good to then do something about it. Of course, that takes the fun out of complaining. I tried to show her how wrong she was by making some limp-wristed attempt to deal with the problem. This usually meant that I would end up looking like the jerk I was, and the problem would be worse than ever. Then I blamed it all on her and murmured silently to myself so she couldn't hear me.

This didn't begin to stop until I recognized that I was a coward. I'd usually let Patti do all the real talking so that she would get into trouble while I sat passively on the sidelines. When I at last saw myself, I asked Jesus to have mercy on me and change my heart. Then, as opportunities arose, I started sticking my neck out a little bit when it seemed that I should. I found that when I walked in obedience, the Lord would protect me from real harm, although not from trouble per se.

A husband will only understand his wife to the extent that he understands his heavenly Father. As with praise and inspiration, understanding is not something we naturally possess. It is something we need to get from God. And with it comes responsibility. The more understanding you have, the more you see in your life that needs changing. A lot of men live in marital bliss, not because they know so much, but because they are so ignorant. That is a bliss of fantasy, however, and sooner or later, reality will catch up with them. The only real way out of our genuine problems is to set ourselves to follow Jesus and do what He says.

Consideration

The next thing I want to talk about is *consideration.*
The Apostle Peter urged husbands to be considerate
of wives and to honor them as heirs equally with themselves of the grace of life. He added that we should
do this so that our prayers might not be hindered (1
Pet. 3:7). That means that we should never make any
significant decision without thinking carefully about
how it will affect our wives. I frequently receive invitations to speak in other churches and at conventions.
In many instances, these meetings are far from home
and would mean that I would be absent for at least a
few days. When I consider my wife's needs and how
my absence will affect her situation, I almost invariably decide against accepting these invitations.

I should add that I consider other things as well—
like the fact that I am a natural-born egomaniac and
that a traveling ministry would probably do me in—
but here I want to emphasize the weight one should
give his wife's needs. Be careful about this, though.
If anyone gets angry at you for a decision you make,
don't turn around and blame it on your wife. You
must make each decision, finally, on the basis of what
you think God wants, and you must take full responsibility for it. And you must be willing to be wrong.

Let's look at this matter in the bedroom. Sam
awakened one morning feeling sexually stimulated
and refreshed after a night's sleep. His wife was still
asleep, but never mind that. After he started making
fairly aggressive sexual advances, however, she did
awake somewhat confused and frightened. Her failure to respond erotically enraged Sam who indignantly
bounded out of bed to get dressed. He later left for

work in a huff, with his wife in tears and his children terrified.

Sam's wife called Patti long distance. "What can I do, Mrs. Williams? I don't know when or if he'll even come home. He may go off and get drunk or find a prostitute. I apologized, but he wouldn't listen—he wouldn't talk about it at all. What can I do now?"

Patti counseled her to stop feeling guilty, that she had committed no sin. Then Patti told her to ask Jesus to protect her from Sam's anger. Then she could pray for Sam that God would touch his heart to help him see his selfishness.

This may seem like an extreme example, but most of us aren't really as considerate of our wives as we would like to think. We naturally regard women as competitors who need to be kept down, so we hesitate to give our wives serious consideration. After all, my wife might take advantage of me if I were too nice. Even if she did, it's not important. God honors obedience.

There is a pseudo-consideration that men, who like to picture themselves as wonderful fellows, offer to their wives. It is a kind of syrupy pretense in which a man proclaims to his wife that he will take care of her as if she were some poor, demented creature who needed a keeper. Here in the South, we're famous for putting our women on pedestals and treating them like pristine goddesses. At the same time, of course, we don't take them seriously as people. The kind of consideration the Apostle Peter talked about, however, meant precisely that we must take our wives very seriously, lest our prayers do not get ready answers.

Service

Number five on our list of things a husband can offer his wife that will cement their love is service. If we take our wives seriously, we'll be ready to be of real service to them. By this I don't mean empty gestures of politeness that are more designed to keep women in their place than anything else.

Mrs. Baldwin was admitted to the hospital as a result of a nervous breakdown. Her husband was an exceptionally selfish man who demanded that he have everything his own way. They had five children who, inspired by their father's example, also insisted on having things their own way. The house was consequently a chaos of conflict. When their fifteen-year-old son didn't get what he wanted for his birthday, he actually broke down the door of his mother's room, assaulted her and threatened her with a gun! Mr. Baldwin handled the situation in such a way that Mrs. Baldwin was unable to tell whether or not the boy had been punished. Not surprisingly, she began to lose control of herself and could not stop weeping. That led to her hospitalization. Prior to that, her husband was so self-centered that he had been unable to see the danger signals and refused to admit that his wife might need professional help.

However, after counseling, Mr. Baldwin began to see that he was largely, if not solely, responsible for his family's predicament. And he began to understand that Jesus was calling him to come down from his lordly throne and take the place of a servant to his wife and children (cf. Matt. 20:27). One of the places this worked out practically and with dramatic effect was in the family's television watching. Formerly, it

75

was everybody for himself, and the disputes among the youngsters over which program would be watched got heated indeed. Mr. Baldwin gave his wife no support in her endeavors to resolve these arguments. She usually ended up screaming and yelling at the kids, and having to leave the room. Now, Mr. Baldwin sees to it that she is no longer burdened by this troublesome task. With a servant's heart, he has apologized to the children for having failed to help them in this matter before. Subsequently, he has worked out a program of TV-watching that is fair to all, and he takes the responsibility to see that it is enforced. This has taught the children, in turn, to work out their problems in other areas on the basis of love rather than selfishness.

C. Northcote Parkinson outlined three characteristics of a true leader—the person who would be number one. One of those characteristics is that such a person does the jobs that no one else in the organization is willing to do. In most places, he said, people assign themselves jobs they like to do, but that always leaves certain jobs that no one likes to do. Such unwanted chores abound in the average household. They include changing diapers, washing dishes, cleaning the bathroom, taking out the garbage and locking up the house at night after everyone is in. Who does most of these jobs in your house? Do you stand aloof from such menial tasks? The answers to these questions should tell you whether or not you have a servant's heart. A servant's time is not his own. It belongs to his master.

Forgiveness

Finally, I want to look at *forgiveness*. Too many of us are deceiving ourselves on this count. We say we have forgiven, when in reality we have only buried our anger where it smolders under the surface. Repressed anger is the source of the cancer that eats incessantly at most marriages.

The reason we get hurt and the reason we hide our anger is *pride*. We have such a high—and unrealistic—opinion of ourselves that even an unintentional slight infuriates us. And because we are so haughty, we refuse to show our anger or even to admit its existence. The joke is on us, though, because we don't fool anyone but ourselves. Everybody else knows.

A lot of men will admit that they don't love their wives anymore, but they won't come clean and admit that they hate them. The closeness of the relationship has broken down the mutual idolatry, and the husband hates his wife because she knows who he is and she is no longer impressed by his propaganda. So, he wants out. He's sure that somewhere, probably at the office, there's a woman who will recognize him for the incredible piece of masculine charm, wit and good looks he actually thinks he is. She'll be swept off her feet by his sexual prowess and his fantastic lovemaking—unlike that "old bag" at home who says it's no fun to make love with such a selfish and angry man. (She may not say it, but her indifference or her "headaches" may spell it out clearly enough.)

What a lot of us men want is a worshiper who will perform the proper rites at our shrine, not a companion with whom to share life on an *equal* footing. No wonder prostitution is the world's oldest business.

Women discovered long ago what men really wanted, and they decided that if they were going to have to put up with this nonsense, the least they could

77

demand in return was some compensation. Any woman who puts up with it in marriage is a victim of fraud, the oldest con-game in history.

Until a man admits that he hates his wife, he cannot begin to love her. And this, in turn, is the key to forgiveness. None of us is capable of forgiving another who has hurt us, apart from the grace of God. But, once we have seen the enormity of our own sin and have received the cleansing of Christ's blood, it is much easier to forgive others. And remember, forgiving your wife is not a matter of feelings, but of choosing. We have to decide to forgive and thus release the offender by an act of our will. This forgiveness is based entirely on the Word of God, which says that we can be forgiven only to the extent that we forgive others (Matt. 6:14, 15). Our relationship with God is conditional upon the confession of our own sins and good relations with His children (James 5:16). We are thus freer to look at ourselves a bit more objectively and even to laugh at ourselves. This reduction in haughtiness places us much closer to forgiving others.

Do you repress your anger until you finally blow your stack? There's another way. *Stop lying to each other, tell the truth, for we are parts of each other and when we lie to each other we hurt ourselves. If you are angry, don't sin by nursing your grudge. Don't let the sun go down with you still angry—get over it quickly; for when you are angry you give a mighty foothold to the devil* (Eph. 4:25-26, TLB).

Patti has helped me immeasurably to mind this Scripture. That is because she is free to tell me when she feels me getting angry. One signal I give off when I'm angry is laughing (it was meant to be a disguise).

Patti has learned to spot it, so that if I laugh at things that should make me angry, she mentions it or asks me if I'm angry. I used to insist that I wasn't, but now I usually offer a quick prayer and ask Jesus to show me my anger. That helps me to start talking with Patti about what's bothering me which leads to new experiences of forgiveness and the grace of God.

Here again are the subheadings of our inventory: praise, inspiration, understanding, consideration, service and forgiveness—six things we can give to our wives that cost us everything and yet nothing. They spell the difference between a marriage that is a matter of *rivalry* or one that is in a place of *revival*.

7

Name Power

Character and Reputation

What do people think of when they hear your name? Do you have any really objective idea? Usually the sound of our own names is music to our ears, but it may not be so with others. Our reputation is based largely on our life-style and how people respond to it. Am I punctual? What kind of language do I use? How do I respond to criticism? What are my obvious goals? What do I spend my money on? Do I have a sense of humor? People who know us, whether well or slightly, have a feeling about us and that is how our *reputation* is formed.

How God feels about us, however, is based on our *character*. Character affects reputation, but the two aspects are seldom identical. People with sterling characters (thanks to the cleansing power of Christ's blood) have frequently had rather bad reputations. Hudson Taylor, the founder of the China Inland Mission, was raked across the coals by the London newspapers for taking women missionaries to interior China in the mid-nineteenth century. In those days, his reputation wasn't worth two cents. But time showed that he was truly a man of God.

Our names have power when we walk in faith and obedience. Remember the story of the seven sons of Sceva who tried to expel demons in the name of Jesus whom Paul preached? It says that the evil spirit answered them by saying, "Jesus I know, and Paul I know: but who are you?" (Acts 19:13-16).

Our names lack power because we are too concerned about what people think or might think. What will the guys at the shop think if I stop making jokes about my wife? Will people think I'm getting too religious? My parents would be angry if I took my family on vacation and didn't go to see them.

The power that might otherwise accompany our names is further diminished by all the bad advice we so readily eat up. The media deluge us with it. After all, the institution of marriage is in obvious trouble. People are looking desperately for help. So people write books, give lectures, give interviews on television talk shows and broadcast their ideas on the radio. The main problem with most of this advice is that it seeks only to save marriages and does not go to the root of the problem in terms of our idolatry and rebellion. Thus, these efforts are little more than Band-Aids for a gaping wound.

One of the most popular prescriptions for curing marital ills going around today involves ways that married couples may reintroduce pleasure into their relationship. Gourmet dinners and erotic games often constitute the framework for this plan. There's nothing wrong with those things, per se. What I object to, however, is the sense in which this becomes a prescription for renewing idolatry between a husband and wife wherein they mutually agree to admire and flatter one another. It is, admittedly, a tempting possibility for the woman who feels trapped in her suburban, middle-class home—and for the husband who feels unappreciated. Why not make the best of a bad deal?

But that is not God's way of restoring order and vitality to the home. Any husband who encourages his wife to follow this course is very short-sighted. It will lead nowhere and ultimately the real problems of marriage will only become more snarled because of the need to drive back out of the dead-end street.

What we must face squarely is that God is not primarily in the business of saving marriages. Certainly, He meets each of us at the point of our need. He meets students through the crises of their studies, business people through the crises of economics, athletes through the crises of competition, married people through the crises of their families. But where He meets us and where He plans to take us are two different things. His purpose is that the kingdoms of this world shall become the Kingdom of our God and of His Christ, and He "shall reign for ever and ever" (Rev. 11:15). This includes our little kingdoms of self. It is in surrendering our own kingdoms and seeking His instead that our needs are met, purely as a by-product, not as a goal (Matt. 6:31-34).

So we need to find out what is involved specifically in living in the Kingdom of God. Since so many of us picture a kingdom in geographical terms, it might be better to say the reign of God. God reigns— His Kingdom exists—wherever He is obeyed.

One night, at about 10:00, I received a phone call from a young man. His voice was edged with desperation. "Page, can you come over? I know it's late. But my wife and I really need your help."

I don't usually accept such requests, but that night I felt the Holy Spirit nudging me to go right away. I confessed my anger and selfishness at having my evening interrupted, and I asked the Lord to give me grace to help this young couple. I didn't have a clue as to the specific problem they were having since I did not know them that well.

As it turned out, Lawrence, the husband, had slept with a prostitute about six months before, after he had had a fight with Sylvia, his wife. During the succeeding months, his conscience had really been bothering him. Sylvia sensed this and kept probing until he finally blurted out the truth. With that, Sylvia became almost hysterical and Lawrence decided to call me. He knew he was wrong to commit adultery, but confessing it to his wife seemed to make the situation worse.

Behind this incident, I knew, was where the real problem lay. Years of wrong mental attitudes and sin on the part of both husband and wife had led up to this crisis. After giving them time to get out a good portion of their hostilities and fears, and trying to help them get in touch with their real feelings, I ended our midnight conference by briefly outlining what I believed God would do for them. We prayed together, thanking God for this "insoluble problem" and for the opportunity it gave them to learn to lean on Jesus.

As I was leaving, Sylvia looked at me with tears still streaming down her cheeks, "Page, can our marriage work?"

84

"Why, sure! What happened tonight has brought to light many things that were hidden in darkness. That's always a good sign. You two are going to get together with Patti and me for the next few weeks to talk about how God wants your marriage to be. Are you willing to learn?"

They both nodded affirmatively as I walked out the door and said good night.

What Patti and I shared with Lawrence and Sylvia during the weeks we spent together after that night was not "techniques" for a happier marriage, but an introduction to life in the Kingdom (rule) of God. A very handy guide to that can be found in Psalms 15:

> O Lord, who shall sojourn in thy tent? Who shall dwell on thy holy hill? He who walks blamelessly, and does what is right, and speaks truth from his heart; who does not slander with his tongue, and does no evil to his friend, nor takes up a reproach against his neighbor; in whose eyes a reprobate is despised, but who honors those who fear the Lord; who swears to his own hurt and does not change; who does not put out his money at interest, and does not take a bribe against the innocent. He who does these things shall never be moved.

To sojourn in God's tent or dwell on His hill is another way of saying to live in His Kingdom or under His reign. The Psalmist lists God's answer to his question under five general headings. What this gives us is the picture of a person who has repositioned himself under God. You don't set out to do these things in order to attain godliness. Instead, once you have surrendered and you keep on surrendering your kingdom to God's Kingdom, you will find that you will begin living, at least roughly, according to this picture. And when you see that the list doesn't describe you in one or more particulars, it's time for confession and repentance. You've been fooling yourself about something, saying that it was under the Lordship of Christ when it wasn't.

The first category presented by this picture speaks of blamelessness, uprightness and honesty. Those are mighty big words. Who among us would dare say he was blameless, that he always did right and was honest down to his toes? Only a self-righteous egomaniac would say things like that. Nothing could be more contrary to human nature. But that's precisely the point. These big words are meant to bring us face-to-face with our complete inadequacy. They are supposed to overwhelm our silly pretensions of goodness and make us see who we really are.

Only Jesus ever walked blamelessly, did what was right always and invariably spoke the truth from His heart. That's why He alone can introduce us to such a life and give us the power to live it. Thus, it is that we stop leaning on people, especially our wives, and begin leaning on God and His everlasting arms. And we stop blaming others when things go wrong. We lose our fear of reality and don't collapse in the face of rebuke and criticism, but are able to listen with an increasing degree of objectivity. We become occupied with Christ rather than being preoccupied with ourselves.

I remember once when I was talking with a particular man. He had been a heavy drinker and smoker. Then he became converted, attended church incessantly, and no longer drank or smoked. After five years, however, he fell back into his old ways. I noticed that he used the word "trying" a lot. He was *trying* not to drink or smoke. He was *trying* to be a good husband. It became obvious that he was trying instead of trusting. That meant he was preoccupied with himself and not with Christ. He wanted to be righteous in his own power and not in the power of Christ. I told him that he needed Christ's righteousness—his own way was only getting him deeper into his problems.

None of this new life emerges overnight. It's a little-by-little process, precept by precept. But in time, it will mean that you will become the sort of man any woman would love to be married to.

The man with the drinking and smoking problem needed desperately to get out of himself and into Christ. His wife was running around on him, and he was *trying* (there's that word again) to win her back by *trying* to be very good. Ugh! He didn't want to see himself as a sinner, but as a victim or a martyr. Nevertheless, he was suffering because of his own sin, and that suffering was motivating him to give up his sin (cf. 1 Pet. 4:1-2).

Living Without Secrets

An honest man learns to live without secrets. He grows toward total transparency in all his relationships (learning, of course, how to walk circumspectly before his enemies), but especially in his relationships with his wife and children. One of the problems of an idolater is that he often mistakes his enemies for his friends while he treats his real friends—like his wife—as if they were his enemies. It doesn't make sense.

An honest man loves the truth. Be assured that however painful it may be, truth will not hurt him, but help him. People go crazy trying to hide things in their lives. They live in constant dread of being found out and must especially avoid intimate relationships. Real marriage is thus impossible for a hidden person.

An honest man confesses his sins aloud. He knows perfectly well that he is a sinner and makes no bizarre claims about how the blood of Christ has brought him into sinless perfection. That kind of talk only comes from the fantasy of idolatry.

One time my wife was counseling with a woman over the phone. She explained that her husband was reading *Do Yourself a Favor: Love Your Wife*, and he had told her that the book was for non-Christians and that it didn't really apply much to him, since, as a Christian, he was nearly perfect. Thus, he beat his wife with his self-righteousness, which hurts as badly as being beaten with fists. Christ did instruct us to be perfect (Matt. 5:48), but the sense of the word in the Greek New Testament, *teleioi*, is of maturity and completeness, not pristine sinlessness.

I spoke a moment ago about the different ways in which a man treats his friends and his enemies. The third verse of Psalms 15 deals with this matter in greater detail. It speaks of slander, doing evil to a friend and reproaching a neighbor.

Slandering one's wife is almost a national pastime. But the husband who is maturing and learning to live in the Kingdom of God will begin to regard his wife less and less as his chief enemy. And, as he begins

increasingly to value her as a gift from God, slander
will disappear like fog under a hot morning sun.

Anger is not necessarily a bad thing. It is a response, of which God made man capable, that serves
to protect. The question is, what are you trying to
protect? If it's your own kingdom, then your anger
will come out as sarcasm, hatefulness, teasing, slander and the like. Under the reign of God, it's different. Anger gives direction and power to our acts of
obedience, but it does not injure or terrorize.

Living in the Kingdom of God is a complete re-
orientation. And this matter of friendship is crucial.
When we're in the kingdom of self, we get everything
backwards. So we need God to show us who our real
friends are. For one thing, as long as we're serving
ourselves, we're under God's judgment, and that
means we'll be subject to our enemies. Only after we
come under God's protection do we have a real
chance to have genuine friends—people who will love
us enough to tell us the truth rather than flatter us
with lies.

Like slander, doing evil to one's friends doesn't
happen once we learn who our friends really are and
to value them as gifts from God. True friends are very
hard to find. You have to be a little bit crazy to do
evil to them, but that's what idolaters do.

Not only does a mature husband avoid initiating
evil against his wife, he refuses the pressure to join
in when others start backbiting their wives. But a husband who fears his wife as a rival will be ready to believe anything he hears. I once knew a fellow who
listened to his mother tell him that his wife was too
friendly with her boss. Obviously, his mother was
very idolatrous toward her son. As far as she was

concerned, he could do no evil—he was her boy. This fellow's wife, on the other hand, loved him enough to hold down a job and run their house, and that kind of competence really threatened her husband. Subsequently, solely on the weight of his mother's malicious gossiping, he went down to see his lawyer in order to start divorce proceedings.

Another husband had a wife who loved Jesus and had learned to be very honest. A lot of people were jealous of the way God used her. They especially despised her for her forthrightness. Her husband was jealous, too, and he started listening to his enemies who told lies about her. It almost destroyed his marriage until he woke up and saw what he was doing.

The minute you feel even slightly pleased when you hear other people picking out the flaws in your wife's character, you are headed for disaster! That disaster will come from God as a judgment on your sin.

A godly husband not only doesn't take up a reproach against his wife, he refuses to allow others to do so when it's within his power. When it is appropriate, he will defend her in her absence. He will especially oppose her parents and his own whenever they seek to defame her. This is certainly a consequence of the biblical directive that a man should *leave* his father and mother in order to *cleave* unto his wife. Before he enters wedlock, a man must be ready to become emotionally and financially independent of his parents.

In the fourth verse of Psalms 15, we learn the difference between the way a godly person regards reprobates and the way he views God-fearing people. A lot of this has to do with what we've already discussed, the difference between friends and enemies.

An idolater inevitably has the matter backwards. He honors the reprobates and despises those who fear the Lord. That is because he doesn't evaluate people on the basis of their relationship to God, but on the basis of how much they flatter and seem to love and honor him as the "god" he thinks he is.

The only safe way to tell the difference between these two types of people is to look at the fruit of their lives and see what it tells you about how they love God. Every other kind of criterion is bound to mislead you sooner or later. The way a person dresses, talks or carries on his business will tell you something about him. His taste in music, books, literature and art will also tell you something. But none of these is conclusive, and they don't necessarily tell you about how a person feels about God. Yet, how often do we pick our friends and honor—or despise—them on account of these kinds of things?

To have a God-fearing wife is to possess a jewel without price. To ridicule any wife who is seriously seeking to know God is the act of a fool. What we want to aim for instead is the emotional maturity to be able and willing to help our wives draw nearer to Christ. This means correcting our wives when we see them in error. Most of us would rather let them go down in flames because that would secretly please us and make us feel like we were on top. Correction between a husband and wife must be a shared activity. The reason we don't want to share is because we don't want to be corrected.

He *swears to his own hurt and does not change.* Do you keep your promises until it turns out that it will work a hardship on you? What would happen if you told your wife you would be home at 6:00 for dinner, and you got involved in some very friendly small talk with your boss at 5:15? Would you break it off, even if your boss might be offended?

If you told your son you would take him fishing on Saturday, would you turn down the opportunity for overtime that would get some back bills paid in order to keep your promise to your son? I had one husband tell me that he never makes promises, because he doesn't know if he can keep them. That seemed like a cop-out to me. We should be careful about what we promise, but we should always do what we promise.

I watched a television drama one night that strongly affected me personally. It was the story of a young policeman who was very ambitious and working hard for a promotion. Morning after morning, the policeman's little son would listen to him promise his wife that he'd be home in time for dinner, but it seldom ever happened. Finally one night, when he should have been home but was working overtime, his wife was murdered in their apartment by some teen-aged hoodlum.

The little boy was intensely angry at his father and wouldn't speak to him. When other officers talked to him, it was obvious that he held his dad responsible for his mother's death. And he called his father a liar. It finally worked out between them, but I couldn't help but be impressed by the little son's perception of his father. It really struck me. For years, I had made a practice of telling Patti I'd be home early. I did it not because I intended to be home then, but because I didn't want any arguments from her before I got out of the house. The truth was, I came home when I pleased without much regard for Patti's needs. And

I certainly didn't regard my own words. I was a "liar" in that sense. Also, I was not a very good example for my children.

A man I know who does a lot of prison-visitation work once told me that almost every inmate with whom he had talked had a bad image of his father. Most of them have been so disappointed by their fathers that they are very suspicious of all authority figures. As a result, my friend makes a practice never to promise inmates anything he is not sure he can deliver. For example, if one of them asks him to correspond with him, he tells them that he is a poor letter writer and that it might take a couple of weeks to answer. We dads could all take an example from that kind of honesty.

One of the complaints I often hear from men is that their wives don't trust them. Of course, most of us have such high opinions of ourselves that it never occurs to us that we might indeed be untrustworthy. If your wife doesn't trust you, ask Jesus to show you why. Don't just assume that it's because your wife is blind to your virtues.

Handling Our Money

This brings us to the last verse in Psalms 15. *The man who lives in God's tent* [presence] *now, does not put out his money at interest, nor does he take a bribe against the innocent.* The way we handle our money, the purposes to which we apply it and what we will do to get it tells a lot about us.

We men often tend to put a lot of pressure on our wives through money, so much so that they feel oppressed. We may feel that because we bring home the bacon, or some share of it, which these days could be a lot less than our wives bring home, that we're entitled to just about whatever we want because we have a misconception of what the "head of the home" really is. We want our money back with interest, so to speak. This gets back to whether you regard your wife as a rival to subdue or as a companion with whom to share. If the former, you will most likely propagandize her with the idea that she's driving you into bankruptcy. This instills guilt, a powerful medium by which to oppress and control people in general and your family in particular.

The other side of this is the wife who is indeed spending money disastrously. Any husband faced with this reality had better find out quickly why his wife is doing it. It may be that she's angry about something and has decided that money is the only way she can get back at you or get your attention. Many times people who feel depressed find that buying themselves something gives them a little lift. If you don't "really love" your wife in truth, and she's not the sort to go out and commit adultery to try to find love with another man, you may discover that she's finding her solace by purchasing things. Obviously the solution to such a problem, once you discover it, is not punishing your wife by taking away her credit cards. Instead, ask Jesus to show you how to love your wife as your own body so that you can continue doing yourself a favor.

Money is a status symbol, a measure of success. As such, it feeds our idolatry very readily. The person who becomes absorbed with money per se is "greedy," but he is seldom rich. Most rich people got that way by doing something they enjoyed and doing it well.

Money was not their objective, but merely a by-product of their *work!*

Greediness always leads to oppression. Sometimes it goes to extremes, as with the imprisoned bank robber whom a friend of mine had once counseled while visiting the prison. The inmate told him he knew something that was much better than Christianity.

"Please tell me about it," replied the counselor.

"It's money, man."

"Is that right?"

"Yeah, I'm talking big money, like 20,000 dollars a week," he explained with his eyes aglow. "But you wouldn't know anything about that kind of money."

"Don't be too sure," the counselor rejoined. "God blessed me one year with over a million dollars."

"Hey, man, don't put me on."

"It's true. But I can tell you something even better."

"What's that?"

"God has blessed me with a lot of money, but during the last year and a half, I've lost over two million dollars!"

"Man, if I lost that much money, I'd die," gasped the inmate. "Don't tell me that. It's bad news."

"All right, now I'll tell you the good news! You said that you would die if you lost all that money. But I lost it, and I didn't die. In fact, because of Jesus in my heart, I have peace about the whole matter—I even feel joyful. I think that proves that Jesus is better than money."

Not that day, but later, that convict decided Jesus was better and today he is a believer in Jesus and lets Him fulfill all his longings.

Money is power. Without money, many of us feel as if we're powerless, worth absolutely nothing. It is a real conversion to turn away from the worship and love of money to the worship and love of Jesus.

Many husbands mistakenly think that they are proving their love for their wives and families by paying the bills. And they think that their munificence entitles them to the love and adoration of their family.

"I work my tail off to provide my family with conveniences, but they don't appreciate it," Steve snarled at me across my desk.

"Be honest, Steve," I said. "Are you really working for your family or for yourself?"

"We never had anything in my family when I was growing up," he whined, "so I vowed to myself that my wife and children would never have to go without the way I did. And I'm making sure they don't. They have every convenience money can buy!"

"Listen to yourself, Steve. It's for yourself you're doing this. You're trying to make it up to yourself for what you think you missed in childhood. And you probably did miss something, but it was love and not money. Do you think giving your wife lots of clothes and things and your children lots of toys will prove that you love them? Did you ever ask them if they would rather have the conveniences or your personal time and attention?"

"Steve, I think you know you haven't got any love to give them, and you're trying to disguise that fact with all those conveniences you provide. Stop denying. Jesus can help you. Confess your need and ask Him, and He will provide."

There are a group of men, on the other had, who feel guilty about having money. For whatever reason, it suits their purposes to be without money. (This is often a means to feed self-pity in what I call the martyr complex.) Of course, this man's wife and children suffer cruelly. He usually doesn't make enough money, and what he does make, he does not spend wisely. On top of that, he makes himself and others believe he is doing it in the name of Jesus.

But I believe that a husband can do more good with money than without it. How much he has is not important. What is important is whether he lets God have control of it, 100 percent. A godly husband, under the direction of the Holy Spirit, is a powerful instrument to proclaim the name of Jesus.

Our attitude toward money also determines what we will or will not do to get it. *Taking a bribe against the innocent* is the act of a cruel and selfish man. Most of us are not judges in courts of law that we might be subject to this temptation, but there are lesser affairs in which we have to decide between contending parties. For example, when our children are warring against their mother, do we remain passive or do we take the matter in hand in order to defend our wives? Are we willing to favor a child or even a stranger for the sake of a little cheap flattery? Often daughters can curl their daddies around their fingers and thereby discomfit their mothers. When that happens, is the father not taking a bribe against the innocent wife?

On a broader plane, how we make our money deeply affects the quality of our marriage. If a man cheats at work, or otherwise defrauds his employer, or cheats on his income tax, it means he will have a bad conscience which, if unattended, will shipwreck his faith. Since it's impossible to have a truly successful marriage apart from the grace of God, and since it is by faith that we receive that grace, it stands to reason that

97

a man who gets his money deviously is headed for trouble maritally as well as otherwise.

We could talk on at great length about all these matters, but I hope that, in reviewing Psalms 15, I have at least sketched some of the specific areas of life that show just how well we know God and how we can employ fully the power of His name. Until we give primary and exclusive priority to the rule of God in our lives, we can never even begin to experience that power on a consistent basis. But once we do, the possibilities are unlimited. It is an adventure in the best and highest sense.

8

Peace at Any Price

Bill and Charlene had been married fifteen years when they first came to see us. They had a thirteen-year-old son and nine-year-old daughter. In recent years, Charlene had gotten involved in two different extramarital affairs. She and Bill were bewildered by this because they had had such a peaceful marriage. They assured us that they had never fought.

That sounded an alarm for both Patti and me. Marriage means conflict—there's no way around that. So, if a couple tells us that they never fight, we believe them, but we know that something is seriously wrong in their marriage. It means that neither partner is being honest. Both are so emotionally immature that they are willing to sacrifice truth and commitment—and a lot of other valuable ingredients for a successful marriage—for the sake of peace and quiet. That is too high a price to pay.

But that kind of peace is illusory. It is actually more like a narcotized state than anything else. It is the peace of an infant whose diapers are freshly changed and whose tummy is full. It is not a peace that grown ups can realistically expect to experience.

Both Bill and Charlene had tried to hide from their own feelings and from one another. For more than ten years, they were sure they had succeeded. They never argued, but the stress of the cold war was really more debilitating in the long run than a hot one would have been. Buried resentments turned Charlene into a frigid woman (with her husband at least). But her sexual drives did not know that and her hormones continued to flow at predictable rates. Adultery presented itself as the perfect solution. It satisfied her subconscious rage against Bill and her sexual impulses at the same time. Of course it was no solution at all, but it finally served to bring the conflict out into the open where it could be dealt with. But if either Bill or Charlene had been more emotionally mature, the adultery probably would never have occurred. As it was, they were two people who were each completely sold out to false images of themselves as wonderful, peace-loving, easy-to-get-along-with kind of folks. That's idolatry.

The real road to peace for Bill and Charlene lay in their getting in touch with their own feelings, recognizing themselves, in turn, as egomaniacs and asking Jesus to have mercy on them. They needed to renounce the lie that peace must be had at any price and to embrace the truth that peace can only be had under the Lordship of Jesus Christ in the midst of conflict. That is why Paul called it the peace that is beyond our capacity to understand (Phil. 4:7).

As is our pattern, Patti and I focused our attention on Bill. It made plenty of sense because he was the "innocent" party and trying to be very nice about it.

100

This showed that he was still in denial and out of touch with reality, much more so than his wife who had at least expressed her feelings, no matter how clumsily.

We tried to help him see that he, too, was responsible for his wife's misdeeds. Had he been walking uprightly and speaking the truth in love as the head of his wife under Christ, we were positive that Charlene would not have started finding the men at her office so attractive. That certainly does not let Charlene off the hook. But, in fact, she was already hooked by her blatant sin. As long as Bill, however, only saw himself as a victim, he was not going to be able to come to Christ, the Savior of sinners.

It was hard, but God helped Bill see the truth. And, when he began to listen to and obey God, that marriage began to defrost under the warmth of God's love. Once that frozen lake was thawed, it often looked pretty turbulent. But that's only because water is more responsive to wind and tempest than is ice.

Reality and Responsibility

Once a husband begins to live in reality and take responsibility for his family, he will almost certainly see himself as being subjected to impossible demands. When that happens, he takes a big fall into self-pity (repressed anger) and sulks. It's just a Mexican standoff on the part of his self-life, though, and if he's willing to choose Jesus rather than himself, he can readily be lifted out of his self-dug pit. Then he can face the fact that the responsibility of his family is impossible. There's no way he'll be able to shoulder it successfully. But this time he'll know to turn to Jesus for help.

Turning to Jesus introduces a person to upside-down and inside-out *living!* Actually it's right-side-up, but since most folks are still trying to live by their own strength—as if they were God—the way of Jesus looks upside-down at first. Once you've tried it for awhile, however, you'll feel a relief and accompanying peace that will assure you that you've turned right-side-up for the first time in your life. Gone will be that uneasy feeling that you were hanging by your heels and might crash to the hard surface below at any moment.

I've already discussed the way of Jesus as the way of the cross—life achieved through death—so I won't belabor that point again. What I want to say to you is don't be disturbed over the tremendous responsibility you have as a husband and a parent. You can shift the burden to God if you're willing to cease being a lord and take on the role of a steward, someone who takes care of another person's possessions. God's ownership of what you previously considered your property may hurt your pride, but it will save you from a nervous breakdown. So reposition yourself—become a steward. Stewardship is the recognition of God's ownership of all that you are and have.

Once in that place, a man is surprisingly freer to stop blaming his problems on other people. He can also give up his dependence on other people, or liquor or institutions. And he can actually hear godly advice and receive it from his wife and other real friends. When problems arise, he can see them as God's warnings and judgments on his sin. If his kids get into trouble, he asks the Holy Spirit to show him why and then what to do about it. He does not assume that he knows what to do, but always looks to God for wisdom.

The man who lives like this has tremendous resources available to him. In addition to the wisdom that the Lord promises to those who ask for it (James 1:5), protection from one's enemies is at hand. By this a godly husband can avoid the plots of covetous people and even the ravages of inflation.

But all of this involves the discipline of standing against ourselves and in favor of Jesus. Discipline is not pleasant, yet it yields the peaceable fruit of righteousness. The great discipline of marriage is the mutual submission between a husband and wife. Many teachers have emphasized the submission of the wife to her husband, but have overlooked the mutuality of this submission. Paul begins his remarks about the husband-wife relationship with the sweeping statement, "Be subject to one another out of reverence for Christ" (Eph. 5:21). All that follows in the succeeding twelve verses is meant to amplify that statement, not to contradict it.

A husband's love for his wife will mean that he can and does submit to her. For example, if a man is having problems with overeating, he would be very wise to submit to his wife's discipline in the matter. For as long as it took, she could decide what and how much he could eat. In a broader sense, he should be generally attuned to her correction and admonition in every sphere of life. A wise man will never suppose himself to be such an expert in any field that he doesn't need advice or correction from his wife. When a wife's advice seems wrong or difficult to understand, the husband should ask God to show him the truth. But he shouldn't ever despise her remarks as worthless. That is the suicidal act of a male egomaniac.

By the same token, a mature husband will love his wife enough to correct and admonish her as well.

Many men don't do this (1) because they enjoy the role of martyr and victim, which they sustain in their fantasy by receiving their wives' correction, but never giving any, or (2) because they're afraid that if they did correct their wives, their haughtiness and competition might show. Others just want peace at any price. But it all amounts to a lack of the right sort of love for themselves and a subsequent disclaiming of their wives.

Many automobile accidents occur during the morning rush-hour traffic and involve husbands who are angry with their wives. The advice columns often urge wives to be sweeter to their husbands and to give them what they want—usually sex—so as to reduce accidents. But that only acknowledges that men are big babies and places no demand on them to grow up. No truly loving wife would do that anyway. It's not impossible for a childish man to grow up. Any wife who thinks that it is impossible has fallen into the sin of despair and should repent. With God, all things are possible (Matt. 19:26).

So what did you rush out of the house angry about? If you had really cared about yourself, you'd have gone back in and gotten it off your chest rather than driving recklessly. Maybe your wife was guilty of unloving behavior. Tell her what you feel without insisting that you're right. If there's any truth to what you say, God will authenticate it. But always be ready to be the wrong one. If you tell your wife what's bothering you, she may tell you what's really bothering her. Then you may find yourself staring at your own sin—in cinemascope and technicolor! If you went into it in self-righteousness and pride, that will be a tremendous blow. But if you went into it as a sinner (one who is wrong) with humility, seeking God's reign, then you can welcome the sight of your sin as an answer to prayer.

By the way, I have been using the word "mature" in a sense that might lead some people to believe that maturity is something one can attain. Well, yes and no. Certainly in our appraisals of our friends and acquaintances we regard some as mature and some as immature. But in God's eyes maturity is a never-ending process. If you stop maturing, you are as good as dead. The difference between the mature and the immature (the godly and the wicked, the upright and the crooked) is in the direction in which they are moving with a willingness to see the truth. And anyone who regards himself as having attained maturity in any other sense is in great danger (1 Cor. 10:12).

Making choices and decisions is part of everyone's life. Some decisions should be made quickly, others should be postponed until as many facts as possible can be gathered. But the person who is incapable of making any decisions is in serious trouble and probably needs professional help. A maturing husband who is walking in Christ will face his need to make decisions in dependence on God. That means he asks the Lord to show him what to do. He refuses to lean on his own understanding, but trusts the Holy Spirit's guidance.

When a child asks you if he or she can stay up a little later to watch a favorite television show, don't assume that you know the answer. Send up a quick prayer asking the Lord to help you. After all, only He knows for sure whether this particular show on this particular night is right for your particular child.

In making our decisions, we'll be greatly helped

to hear God's voice if we're familiar with biblical principles. For instance, if you'd like to have a glass of beer, it would be good to know that this is not explicitly forbidden by the Scriptures. Drunkenness is forbidden. And we are enjoined not to offend fellow Christians whose consciences might make them feel that they should never drink anything alcoholic. Reformed alcoholics might especially fit this category. Then, too, you'll want to consider why you want a beer. Since alcohol is a big problem in America, many Christians refrain from alcoholic beverages even though they may not object to them in principle.

A friend of mine once dined with a noted Christian leader who came from a European background. This man was having roast beef and asked if he might have some vinegar. When it was brought to the table, he sprinkled it liberally on his meat. My friend couldn't resist asking him why. "Well," he explained, "because I have trouble digesting it otherwise. But here in America people object so strongly to drinking that I don't touch the stuff. To aid my digestion, I use this vinegar. It does just about the same job."

God is not primarily interested in whether or not you drink a beer, but in whether or not you trust and obey Him. If this question of drinking is of such great importance to you that it is difficult to hear God's voice with any degree of detachment, then you have a problem. It means that your feelings and motivations when it comes to what you drink are especially strong for some reason. It would be helpful to discover that reason. You might learn a lot about yourself and what is keeping you from the full experience of the power of Jesus' name. If you're in doubt about the true reason, ask Jesus to show you.

There are a number of areas of dispute, like drinking, that especially plague marriages, so I want to devote the next chapter to five of the most important bones of contention in any family: religion, sex, finances, in-laws and recreation.

9

Bones of Contention

God's Perspective

There used to be a rule that people weren't supposed to discuss sex, politics or religion on polite social occasions. They were correctly regarded as being too inflammatory for affairs designed with congeniality as the top priority. Today, however, people talk about little else, almost no matter where they are.

I'd like to start this chapter by talking about religion. Our society is increasingly, if not predominantly, pluralistic. One's religious or racial background, for example, no longer dictates whom he or she will marry. Protestants, Catholics, Jews, secularists, blacks, whites—they're all marrying each other. Still, tensions exist in any pluralistic marriage. They may be subtly expressed, but they are nonetheless strong. What to do about them is extremely perplexing to most people, especially since many of them feel vaguely guilty about marrying someone who is not of their religious persuasion.

But the problem will remain hopelessly out of focus until we get God's perspective on it. He sees and fully understands the differences—cultural, religious and racial—that exist between us all. According to the Bible, most of our differences stem, albeit remotely in some cases, from sin (Gen. 11:1-9). God dealt with sin on the cross so that, by the power of the blood of Christ, all our differences can be overcome and we might become one in the Spirit of God. That means that the crucial difference that remains between people involves belief and unbelief. It would be nice (not really) if we could nail down precisely what this means. Then we could neatly label everyone and dispense with individuality. It finally gets down to Paul's assertion, "The Lord knows those who are His, and let every one who names the name of the Lord depart from iniquity" (2 Tim. 2:19). We will never be able to label the elect. Our desire to categorize people is only a symptom of our desire to be God. Thus, we must welcome every person who says he is a believer unless and until the fruit of his life shows otherwise (Acts 8:9-24).

With God's perspective, the focus clears so that we can see how much we need to rely on His guidance and not on our own understanding. A man wrote a letter once to ask my opinion about his problems. He and his wife had come to a living faith in Christ after spending years in their family church. The church was not a cult, and it did acknowledge the deity and Lordship of Christ. He wanted to leave this church and join one that was more evangelical. His wife, on the other hand, was satisfied to remain. She believed that their submission to the authority of the old church would please God. What should he do?

Obviously, I could not answer his question. Only God could tell him what to do. But I suspect, from the tone of his letter, that God is not primarily interested in what church this man attends. That is an outward matter. What is important is the state of his heart. Is it hard with self-righteousness or is it soft with humbled obedience? Until that is settled, there's no point in getting all excited about switching churches. An outward move cannot guarantee an inward change. In fact, there must be the inward change for the matter to be settled in the light of God's Word.

A man who would truly lead his family as its priest and prophet will be broken in spirit and contrite in heart. He will be the servant of his family, standing in a lowly place both inwardly and outwardly. From there he will shepherd his family to the place of worship that God chooses. His own opinions will have been left behind as he obeys God. Such a leader will honor his wife by listening to her, and he will not take advantage of his position to lord it over her. God, in turn, will honor him and vindicate his choices as leader.

Next I'd like to talk about sex. A lot of husbands have the idea that their wives withhold sex from them when things are not going well. Nonsense! Most women—especially those who are trusting in Jesus and being honest with themselves and their husbands—simply have a hard time responding to husbands who treat them cruelly because of their resentments and immaturity. Big babies don't make great lovers. The secular solution to this problem is to try to thaw out the frigid women (not to mention all the impotent men) with some kind of counseling or therapy.

111

It will come as no surprise to you that I want to put the burden of the responsibility on the husband. When our wives don't respond to us, we should not label them as frigid. We should ask God to show us what the problem is. There's a good chance that we're seething inside about something and that our nice-guy front isn't concealing it nearly as well as we might hope. But whatever it is, when you find out, ask God to show you what to do.

It will very likely involve confessing your sin to God and honesty with your wife. It might mean something as simple as being aware of the feelings your wife has of privacy in regard to the children—our timing may be based on our selfish desire to relieve our sexual urge, rather than a genuine love and affection for the precious woman God has given us to love and cherish and respect.

Lusting after other women will damage your relationship with your wife. After you recognize that your fantasizing and flirtation are part of your idolatry (don't those fantasies inevitably involve women who revere us as gods and respond to our amorous advances with delight and excitement?), ask God to help you live in reality and to hate your sin of lust. Let God show you what this really means, and you'll be surprised how those old fantasies lose their sweetness and allure.

I remember how impressed I was when my family and I watched the motion picture, *The Other Side of the Mountain*. It told the true story of a lovely young woman named Jil Kinmont. Jil was an excellent skier and was preparing for the winter Olympics when she was injured in a fall that left her paralyzed from the neck down. The once-vigorous athlete became almost totally helpless, confined to a wheelchair for the rest of her life. And life, which had once seemed so promising, now offered only the bleakest horizon.

However, Jil's boyfriend—also an excellent skier—proved to be a very gallant fellow. After her accident, he proposed marriage to her, assuring her that he was entirely serious. He was not grandstanding to look noble and heroic. He was, he said, deeply in love with Jil as a whole person.

I was thrilled to see depicted on the screen a young man with such maturity. Sexual enjoyment, per se, was going to be pretty limited between them, yet he made his decision knowing that love does not depend on sex for its fruition. It will tell us a lot about our love for our wives if we can honestly ask ourselves how would we feel about them if sex were not possible.

The man who asks God to teach him how to love his wife will learn the truth that his sex life goes in the way he makes it go "in love." He will see sex as sacramental and his wife as a person with needs like his own. He will want to protect and cherish her as he assumes responsibility for her sexual fulfillment. And surely the woman who feels such authentic warmth and caring will be wonderfully responsive to her husband. The point is that a man can't fake this kind of thing. If the Holy Spirit doesn't make it work, it won't work.

Money is a constant source of contention between many husbands and wives. We've already discussed the various reasons for that in chapter seven. Here I want to talk about the kinds of things a husband will do with finances if he is learning to love his wife.

First of all, he will bring the firstfruits of all he makes to God. For most of us, this will probably mean tithing our weekly gross income to our church.

He believes in the principle of sowing and reaping—that what he gives away in obedience to God will come back to him multiplied in God's time and in God's way.

Secondly, he pays his taxes honestly with a glad and grateful heart. For most of us, this is a test only once a year when we file our returns because our wages are subject to withholding. But whenever we must perform tasks that bear on our taxes, we should remember that government has divine sanction and that taxes are collected with the authority of God (Rom. 13:1-7). If we object by saying that much of our own government is corrupt and that many foreign governments are despotic, we should remember that Christ and the Apostle Paul inscribed those words to the Roman church which existed under a pagan and harsh set of rulers. We should also remember that a nation generally gets the government it deserves. If we feel that our government is badly run or unfair or whatever, we should look to ourselves to discover the sin that God is judging through the government. Prayers for mercy are more powerful than any political protest (though, if after you pray, God tells you to protest, you should obey).

Once these first two priorities are well established, a husband should begin planning for the financial benefit of his wife and children. In most cases, this will mean an adequate savings program, a will and sufficient life and health insurance programs. The Institute for Christian Financial Planning (Box EG-957, Melbourne, Florida 32935) offers excellent personal counsel nationwide regarding precisely these kinds of matters.

I held a funeral service for a husband and father who died at the early age of thirty-eight. He left behind a wife and five children together with hospital bills, the mortician's bill, a mortgage, consumer debts and a car in need of many repairs. But he did not leave behind a will, nor was there any life insurance. That widow and her children were left entirely dependent on the Social Security benefits. They were cast into near-poverty because of that husband's neglect and, most likely, selfishness.

I want to add a word here for men who are not yet married (if any of you have managed to get this far in a book designed for married men). Proverbs 24:27 says that a man should prepare his fields before he builds his house. I believe that means, for us today, that a fellow would do well to have his income established and his financial affairs in order before he sets out to get married and set up housekeeping. The fact that this is so much at variance with common practice in our society ought to point up just how foolish and selfish most men are. I did not know that verse was in the Bible when I got married, but I was so selfish and immature that, had I known, I probably wouldn't have heeded it anyway.

Now we will turn to the matter of parents and in-laws. A husband's attachments to his parents can pose a real danger to his marriage. He must learn, under God, to free himself from his old life-style in order to follow the pattern God gives him for his own family. Everyone hates the feeling of being alone (some more than others). Most of us avoid loneliness by being in a family. But it's still lonely to be the head of a family. I believe that's why so many men try to abdicate the post in one sense or another. The real solution, of course, is not to abdicate, but to relocate under the headship of Christ.

A maturing husband will seek to sever his emotional, financial and psychological dependence on his parents in order to become entirely dependent on his heavenly Father. This may mean a geographical move, but it certainly means refusing to compare your wife to your mother, refusing to make decisions on the basis of what your parents or hers might think and refusing to think of your parents when needs arise instead of listening to God.

In-laws include more than the parents. Many families have strong traditions that bind the family together very tightly. These bonds can be idolatrous in that they make a kind of god of the extended family. You can see this, in its extreme form, in organized crime. But, in its subtler forms, it's commonplace throughout much of the world. As such, it is something that Jesus cut across very sharply (see Luke 12:51-53). Family traditions can insist that children participate in the family business when they grow up, or that they should attend certain schools, participate in certain sports or even marry a particular person. Thought is seldom given, in the observance of these family traditions, as to any conflict with God's will for the person in question. How, for example, could a young person hear God's call to the mission field if he or she were worshiping at the shrine of the family and being called by it to be an apprentice in the family-owned business?

When God calls a person to follow Him, He calls him into a new family. It is no longer his kindred with whom he seeks fellowship and communion. Instead, he finds a more significant relationship with his brothers and sisters in Christ. It is the Holy Spirit that forms the strongest bonds between people, not blood or law.

Family Idolatry

Patti and I have discovered from our counseling that most couples who are having in-law troubles have not been honest with their kin. The husband will tell his wife one thing, his parents another thing and her parents still another. Soon there emerges a tangled mess of deception and hypocrisy—and everyone is angry.

Family gatherings can be times of special stress. The grandchildren are all evaluated so that your wife has to compete with her sister to see which one has produced the cutest and best-dressed and best-behaved children. Then there is the ritual whereby the pecking order is adjusted and reaffirmed—the lowest member is the butt of all the jokes, often subjected to downright cruelty. These are things a godly man would have to oppose in the power of the Spirit in order to protect his wife and children.

Family idolatry can affect all kinds of things. I knew a young couple who were from separate evangelical churches with very similar doctrines. However, they couldn't agree on which church to attend together. She didn't want to join his because she would have to be re-baptized. He didn't want to join hers because his mother would object. Admittedly, they were both being pigheaded, but I'll fault him more. How was he going to discover God's will as the spiritual leader of his wife as long as he was so worried about what his mother would think or act?

But people make decisions all the time based on family wishes. Then they wonder why they have problems. Family idolatry inevitably leads to problems because more than one family is involved—your parents and your wife's parents. If you aim your life to try to please one or the other, you will immediately foster jealousy and competition between them which can lead to really bitter hostility. The only way to safely overcome this treacherous road is to follow Jesus. Even if what He tells you to do makes your parents very angry, He can protect you and even change their hearts. Walking in the Spirit like this is also the only way we can learn the otherwise impossible task of honoring our parents as God commanded while at the same time demolishing the idols of the clan.

How a family does or doesn't spend its leisure time is a big problem in our homes, because leisure has become big business. Most of us spend a fair amount of money on recreation. And some observers have noted that we seem to work even harder when we're involved in recreation than when we're actually making money! This seems to be especially true of middle-class and upper-middle-class, white-collar workers whose jobs are not physically demanding. The man who comes home after a day of digging ditches or being a construction worker is usually not ready for much additional activity. His idea of fun may be sitting in his easy chair and watching a western on television.

The real question, though, is what does a husband have in his heart toward his family when he comes home from work? The average idolater looks forward to his own free time as just that—a time when no one can tell him what to do, a time to indulge his fantasies to their fullest. As such, he is completely bound up in himself, and though he may go through the motions of trying to be a good man, there is really no place in his heart for his wife and children—and, sooner or later, they'll all sense it. Next, resentment will begin to build. Then he'll wonder why they're so unappreciative when he does special things for them. Because he sees himself as a perfectly wonderful fellow, it will not occur to him that he makes every family outing a bleak affair simply by being there!

When two idolaters marry each other, they will often seek to sustain the euphoria of their early days together by a frantic involvement in recreational activities. They may bowl, play cards, swim, play tennis, golf, ride bicycles, blade-skate, snow ski, fish, go boating or do any number of things. The problem is not that they do these things, but that they literally bury themselves in them, strenuously seeking to maintain the old illusions.

Husbands and wives who are idolaters generally regard sexual activity as a matter of recreation. This has to do directly with their fantasies about themselves. In this way their wives are really nothing more than playthings. That is the "Playboy" philosophy. Women are not people; they, like one's sports car or wardrobe, are *things* made to be enjoyed. The look and build of your woman serves to enhance your image as a man of great sex appeal and excellent taste.

Recreation is also an opportunity to escape responsibility and to regress into childhood. Several years ago, when Patti, the children and I were at the beach, Patti had to leave, and she asked me to keep a special eye on Plythe who was then only about three years old. Plythe and I played, making sand castles and splashing in the water. But, after a little while, I got preoccupied with doing broad jumps, something I enjoyed doing as a young boy in elementary school.

When Patti returned, she spotted Plythe almost fifty yards away from where I was. At that very moment, a large wave had just come in and was forcing little Plythe under the water. Patti screamed in terror and I suddenly awoke from my reverie. I sprinted to where she was and retrieved her from the water. She spluttered loudly as she came up and was terribly frightened, but otherwise she was all right. It took a while to calm her down, but it didn't take me long to see myself. Plythe's guardian angel had taken care of her, while her daddy was "playing." I confessed my irresponsibility to God and thanked Him for cleansing me and forgiving me.

The point I'm making is that we need to bring our leisure time under the Lordship of Christ just as thoroughly as any other aspect of our lives. To do this, it might be better to call it "unscheduled," rather than "free," time. We need to give up our rebellious and self-willed ways and to confess the truth that we don't belong to ourselves, but to Christ (1 Cor. 6:20). This isn't easy, and we really need to ask Jesus to help us and change our hearts. By a gradual process, you will then begin to ask the Lord to show you what to do with unscheduled time. Of course, you can tell Him what you want to do with it, and there's a fair chance He'll tell you to go ahead. But we should always be aiming for the time when we will hunger and thirst for His perfect will.

In my own experience, I've found considerable enjoyment and refreshment from getting odd jobs done around the house in my spare time. I was surprised to find how happy I felt after fixing a leaky faucet or mowing the lawn or spraying the shrubs when I found some unscheduled time and asked Jesus what to do with it rather than deciding what I wanted. For one thing, it kept me from that uneasy feeling I would get whenever I started a project and worried about other things that weren't getting done. But now, when I trust God to let me know what to do—and He often tells me to do things I've been postponing or otherwise trying to avoid—I find I'm largely free from that uneasy feeling because I know God is in charge and He'll tell me when to do those other things.

Another thing I've learned to enjoy—as Jesus has changed my heart—is shopping with my wife. I know a lot of wives say they would rather shop alone, but that's because we husbands are such miserable companions that we invariably turn a pleasant shopping trip into a dismal drudge. Confess your self-centeredness and ask Jesus to change your heart. You'll find yourself genuinely excited at the prospect of shopping with your wife—because you'll be with her.

Husbands find a lot of things boring if those things do not tend to feed their idolatry. Church socials, reading good books and quiet dinner parties don't fit in with their macho fantasies of heroic deeds and sexual exploits. It's amazing how much more fun you can have in life once you learn to laugh at yourself and get off the throne of the universe.

Thank God for these bones of contention. Without them, we might live on in our little dream worlds forever. Instead, our conflicts awaken us to our need of Jesus and, thus, to a whole new dimension of living.

10

New Life for Your Marriage

Is your wife a widow? Are your children orphans? "Of course not!" you reply. But wait a
minute. Let's think about those questions a little harder. Just how alive are you? Are you really able to
love your wife and children? What is the quality of
life you bring into your home?

The Bible says that, apart from Christ, we are dead
in trespasses and sins (Eph. 2:1). That's something to
take more seriously than we often do. Being dead
isn't always a matter of brain waves and heartbeats.
Death denotes separation and absence of life, but life
is more than biological existence. Apart from certain
qualities—like compassion, tenderness, courage and
the like—life can be a bleak affair.

Arlene and Marty got married when she was just
out of high school. He was tall, blond, handsome and
about five years older than her. He looked like a real
"savior," for she longed to get away from an unhappy home. But it wasn't long after their wedding that
she began to recognize that Marty was married to his

job. They bought a rundown house that she tried to fix up while Marty spent long hours at work. Whenever she complained, he protested that he had to do it in order to become successful. When he came home, all he did was eat and fall asleep in front of the television.

Arlene hoped that the birth of their child would bring new life to their dying marriage, but it didn't. Now there was an orphan in addition to the widow. Arlene grew sullen and resentful, and she began to eat. Soon she was quite overweight, and Marty managed to stay at work for longer and longer hours.

Later, Arlene lost their second child at birth. It was a crushing blow, but she was a strong woman. The grinding process continued for another two years. It was that summer that Arlene's parents invited her and her child to accompany them on a long vacation. It was an exhilarating time for her and renewed her faith that she could make their marriage work. She even took off fifty pounds. She was looking and feeling much better. She called Marty often to tell him of her hopes, but he was noncommittal. And, when she got home, he told her that he had discovered that he could live as well without her. Therefore, he was offering her a chance to get out by asking for a divorce.

The story went on from there. Arlene, crushed by this turn of events, met Jesus in a profound way. He supplied her needs through others—Christians who were able to help her. But I share this story to illustrate how very little we have to offer our wives if we don't have Christ. The best Marty could do without Jesus was to politely offer his wife a divorce. There was nothing better in his heart.

My immediate reaction when I hear a story like
this is to assure myself that I am not like Marty. But
the truth is, I am very much like him. I shared my
testimony in the early chapters of this book so that
you could see how true that is. I was a Christian, too,
or at least I thought so. I certainly was not walking
in the Spirit. Marty didn't even profess to be a believer. As such, I think he was more willing to face
bankruptcy in his marriage than I was. (His chief
fault lay in not being willing to do anything about it
once he saw it.) None of us really has the resources
to sustain a living, loving marriage, and we Christians
are entirely too quick to assume that our relationship
with God is so rich and fruitful that this does not apply to us. We live in denial. Because of this presumption, we persistently refuse to listen to the very thing
God is trying to say to us in order to bring us into the
abundant life He has promised. But we're fanatics
who want to have the abundant life—or at least imagine that we have it—without going through the means
God has prescribed to get it, namely the cross.

If you and I can just stop defending ourselves and
confess our sin of self-protection—if we are willing to
acknowledge—even a little bit—that, in some respect
at least, our wives are widows and our children are
orphans, it will put us in an entirely different position. First of all, we will read the relevant Scriptures
about what God does for widows and fatherless children—and for those who oppress them—(cf. Ps. 68:5-
6; 146:9; Mark 12:40). Then we can realize that God
is angry with us and ready to pour out judgment on
us. Indeed, we may suddenly understand unpleasant things that have already happened in our lives as
His loving judgment is revealed. If we can see this,

we'll be in a position to step down from our self-made pedestals where we stood as heroes demanding medals, to kneel on the common ground as sinners pleading for mercy.

No posture is more repugnant to most of us men, but that is assuredly the only way out of death into life. I don't suppose I'll convince anybody by saying it, though. Only the truly desperate are ready to hear this. But then God in His mercy is bringing increasing numbers of us to desperation. Hallelujah!

Maybe your wife is a widow and your children are fatherless. So, what's new? Nothing, except that you're now willing to look at it. It's not the end of the world. It's the doorway to a new life. Walk through by asking Him to show you what to do after you've received His forgiveness. What works should you perform appropriate to your repentance? People who repented under John the Baptist's preaching asked him for specific advice and he gave it (Luke 3:10-14). Likewise, the Scriptures say that orphans and widows should be visited in their affliction (James 1:27).

In the Bible, the word "visit" is loaded with more meaning than we normally attach to it. If we say that God visits His people, it certainly connotes more than a quiet hour with coffee and cake. It speaks of hearts awakening, of miracles, of dramatic conversions and so much more. For us to visit our wife, whom we've made a widow by not sharing our innermost feelings and thoughts, implies much more than a polite social call. It implies compassion, tenderness and generosity with our time and attention toward her. Are you short on these? That's all right. Jesus can help you. You're only in trouble if you think you already possess those qualities and that you don't need any help to perform your task.

Quality Time

It's not just how much time you spend with your wife and children that counts, but the quality of what you impart to them while you are with them. Some husbands are often away from home and yet their hearts have been truly softened by Christ so that when they are with their families, the life of Christ is imparted to their wives and children. Other husbands are around the house a lot, but their presence constitute little more than a pall of gloom.

Recent headlines announced a wave of pornography involving children. Apparently thousands of young children in the Los Angeles area have participated as subjects in the production of pornographic films. But all across our country today children are growing up subject to every conceivable kind of temptation and abuse. Drugs, alcohol, crime, witchcraft, immorality, unbelief, vandalism and the like are commonplace among America's youth. And much of the blame for this must be laid at the feet of we fathers who do not love the Lord our God with all our hearts, souls, minds and strength. As a result, we do not have any substantial love for anyone. Children who grow up subject to this neglect in homes feel undervalued (having not experienced the genuine love of Christ), and they are certain candidates for all kinds of sin and rebellion.

The Church has acquiesced to this condition to a great degree. Instead of forthrightly challenging our fathers and husbands to stand up like men, we have coddled them as little babies. After all, we tell ourselves, they are so proud and hard—and angry—that any confrontation will likely lead to a very unpleasant conflict. We prefer peace at any price, so we quietly change gears and leave the men alone.

The Church's alternative has been to concentrate its evangelistic efforts on the women and children. They're easier because they're physically weaker than the men. That means a lot of them know what it means to be oppressed. And children are easily bribed with trinkets and tricks.

I don't want to demean the conversion of women and children. God calls whom He will when He wills, and it is always glorious when He does. But I do see a biblical norm where the father acts as a priest to his family, bestowing the blessing of God on his wife and children (Eph. 5:21-33; 1 Cor. 11:3). It is he who should evangelize his family. Instead, the common practice is to get his children into Sunday school or vacation Bible school. Then, through the children, the Church will touch the hearts of their parents until, at last, even old dad joins. We have even found a verse to validate this whole process, "A little child shall lead them" (Isa. 11:6). I don't think that's exactly what Isaiah had in mind when he wrote that, however. When dad follows his entire family into the church, how is he supposed to get the idea that now he should get out in front? It doesn't often happen. The childlikeness which Jesus held up as a prerequisite for entrance into the Kingdom of God (Mark 10:15) certainly didn't include the kind of childishness we men so often regress into when we don't get our way. Children do throw tantrums, but only as long as adults put up with such behavior. It is when they are restrained that children face the reality of their relative weakness. It is that sense of weakness and dependency that Jesus had in mind.

We need to establish a different set of priorities. We must be willing to lock horns with the men, not because they are better than women and children, but because we have neglected them in the past and because they are the key to the beginning of the change necessary to bring our homes and hearts back to *life*. When the Philippian jailer asked Paul and Silas how he might be saved, their answer included his entire household (Acts 16:31). When Peter announced repentance and baptism to the crowd on the Day of Pentecost, he told them that the promise was to them and to their children (Acts 2:39).

I'm not saying this because God needs men—quite the opposite, they need Him. Nor am I saying this because the Church is too feminine. The Church is not too feminine. And even if it were, the antidote would not be to try to make it more masculine. The Church does not need more masculinity or femininity; it needs *godliness*.

Just as the focus of our evangelism has distorted the effect of the gospel, so has it distorted the content of the gospel itself. We actually invite people to receive Jesus in such a way that they get the impression they are doing God a big favor by converting! I guess we get impatient waiting for the Holy Spirit to convict people of their sin, so we downplay sin and tell people more about the abundant life Jesus will give them if they'll only accept Him. What sort of converts can we expect from preaching like that?

The key to successful marriages is not an easy gospel, but the message of Jesus is that if any man would come after Him, he must deny himself and take up his cross and follow Him (Matt. 16:24). We are faced with a disease that calls for strong medicine; nothing else will do. Every husband who sets out to do himself a favor by loving his wife, sets himself to follow Christ into death and resurrection.

Once a person has determined to do that, he will be ready to examine his life and motives in a way he couldn't have done previously. I've been learning to ask myself the following questions, for example, whenever I'm faced with a decision: Will this glorify God? Will this need to be a secret? Where will this decision lead? Will this bring out the "new man in me" or the "old man in me"?

We're supposed to do everything to the glory of God (1 Cor. 10:31). That's a big order, especially if you try to figure all the angles. The key is to realize that nothing you do glorifies God if it is not an act of obedience and trust. That may sound like a big order, but after a while, when doing your own thing has gotten you into enough trouble, you'll be surprised to discover that it is the easier way (Matt. 11:28-30).

Anything that has to be kept secret is immediately suspect. Hiddenness generally speaks of darkness, and darkness speaks of sin. So, if I am facing some choices and one of them would have to be kept a secret if I chose it, I must ask myself why. How would I feel if I had to tell my wife or my boss or my friends about this? If it means that by making this choice I could not walk fully in the light, then I should avoid it like the plague.

When making a decision, I have also learned to try to "wind it all the way out" to see if it might lead to a dead end. This can be tricky because Satan often makes the prospects of certain choices look golden, while the way of Christ can look very dreary until we learn that beyond the cross is the bright dawn of resurrection morning. This fact underlines our need for the Holy Spirit's discernment, and it calls for our own commitment to stand against ourselves and to stay on the side of Jesus.

Finally, I have learned to think in terms of how certain decisions will affect me. I know myself well enough now to see that certain kinds of choices would be very dangerous for me. As I explained earlier, I very seldom accept speaking invitations far from home. This represents my commitment to my family, but it also stems from my recognition that I can be quickly inflated by being the center of attention. That doesn't mean that I should invariably decline invitations to speak, but that I had better be sure it's God who's telling me to go. If I'm not walking in obedience, I cannot be certain of His grace and protection. I can be sure, however, that my old self will be very much in evidence and getting into the same old troubles which caused the suffering that originally drove me to God.

When suffering drives us to God, God always arranges a party to welcome us home (Luke 15:11-24). There is a celebration whenever any person changes his or her mind and decides to allow God to pour out His blessings on them. This fact is the primary source of my hope for the couples who come to Patti and me with their shattered marriages. In most cases, there is no sensible reason for hope. I think most secular marriage counselors would see divorce as the only reasonable solution. And, if it weren't for God's mighty power to save to the uttermost, I would agree with them.

Let me share one final letter with you.

Dear Rev. Williams,

I just finished reading *Do Yourself a Favor: Love Your Wife* for the second time. I felt like you had been peering over my shoulder during my entire married life. It was uncanny. Now I pray that my marriage can be resurrected, but it may be too late. I almost emotionally destroyed my wife and children, and, finally, eight months ago, my wife asked me to leave. Then she sold the house and took the kids to New Hampshire. Before she moved, I was served with a complaint of divorce. We actually sat down with lawyers and worked out a separation agreement and financial settlement. But, after the move, Mary's attitude inexplicably changed. Six weeks ago we talked on the phone for four-and-a-half hours. She had read your book—which her doctor had loaned her—and then she sent it to me. I have since purchased my own copy. Now she no longer talks about divorce and even mentions the day when we get back together. But I'm impatient and frightened. I really need God's help. I solemnly vow, before you and God, that I will pattern my life according to His plan. I only pray that it's not too late for me to change.

I believe it is not too late, either for him or for you or for me. By faith, I see our homes and hearts being made "alive" in Christ. I see great celebrations as men's hearts are turned to God. I see His Kingdom coming to earth, right down to our jobs, our families, our finances, our sex lives, our relations with our in-laws—permeating the entire fabric of our lives.

Glory to His Name!

Afterword

Conflicts, crises and change will necessarily be part of a marriage that is alive and growing. This pattern holds true for life in general. Psychologists have begun to notice that youngsters who undergo a particularly stormy adolescence often grow into adulthood most successfully. So, if you and your wife start getting more honest with one another and yourselves, things will get worse before they get better.

What we need to know, then, is how to enter this conflict and pass through it in such a way that the Kingdom of God will come more fully in our marriages. First, depend and rely on God—not your wife—to take care of you and supply your needs. Second, stop trying to make your wife happy and start trusting to please God through faith and obedience. If you choose to ignore these two warnings and try to hold onto the old patterns, you'll most likely sink—whether or not you get a divorce. If you heed them, you will likely weather the storms that confront us all and emerge from them wiser, stronger and happier.

Epilogue

In reading this manuscript several months after Page transferred from the Church Universal to the Church Triumphant, I felt it needed closure.

When Page and I learned to put God first, family second and vocation third, God transformed our relationship and marriage. We raised two beautiful children together. Perry Scott is a physician in family practice and has married a lovely young lady, Laura, also a physician. Our daughter Plythe followed in her father's footsteps and is now a director of Christian education in a Presbyterian church. She is married to a wonderful young man, Michael, who is pursuing a career in medicine.

Page not only put God first, but learned to love his family. He provided for me financially in his death. He left me a wonderful church family, a wonderful community in which to live. But most of all, he left me memories of a godly and wonderful husband, father, and pastor. In an age where the institution of the family is under tremendous attack, Page

Williams did all he could to promote God's will for the family. He fought the good fight and kept the faith until the end of his earthly life.

To God be the glory.

Patti Williams, D.Min.
Fort Pierce, Florida
1993